THE SUSHI LOVER'S COOKBOOK

Easy to Prepare Sushi for Every Occasion

Yumi Umemura
with **Tom Baker**
Photography by **Noboru Murata**
Food Styling by **Masami Kaneko**

TUTTLE Publishing

Tokyo | Rutland, Vermont | Singapore

contents

Egg-wrapped sushi with mushrooms

THE MAGIC OF SUSHI

Sushi was a special part of my childhood. I remember how my mother used to prepare sushi on my birthday, for school picnics, and on sports festival days. Thick sushi rolls were my special favorite, and their blend of flavors still brings back sweet memories of my school days. Times have changed, but sushi still holds a special place in Japanese culture. Of course, ready-made sushi is now enjoyed as convenient lunch, but homemade sushi made with love, or gourmet sushi made with skill, is still an important part of celebrations and entertaining.

Meanwhile, sushi has become popular worldwide in recent years, and it surprised me to learn that sushi is enjoyed on all sorts of occasions in other countries, even as a party snack or an appetizer at a barbecue. I like that idea.

Sushi made with nontraditional ingredients was once considered improper. However, almost anything can be included in sushi provided that it is prepared in a basically correct way. I'm sure that my Japanese ancestors would be pleased to learn that sushi is loved enthusiastically by people in the rest of the world today, even as its form is evolving.

I was born in Tokyo, but when I was a girl my family moved from Japan to India for several years as part of my father's career. My parents hired a cook and taught him how to make traditional Japanese meals to entertain official guests. But he also prepared Indian cuisine for when the family ate alone. I found it enthralling to watch him blend spices. He did everything by hand, grinding dried leaves and stems into earthy-looking powders and mixing a pinch of this with a dash of that to give our meals their flavor. To me, it seemed like magic.

As a teenager, I attended the American International School in New Delhi. The cooking classes there were a revelation. A typical dish was Campbell's soup and other canned ingredients mixed together in a casserole dish, topped with cheese, and baked. It wasn't exactly haute cuisine, but everything was so speedy and no-fuss that it was almost like another kind of magic.

Later, when I was newly married, my husband and I lived just outside the ancient city of Kyoto, and I delved into traditional Japanese cuisine at a cooking school there. The school was located on Nishiki Street, which has been described as the kitchen of Kyoto. I encountered many ingredients that I had never seen in Tokyo, partly because the food cultures of eastern and western Japan were so different from one another and partly because I was still something of a neophyte at cooking.

To be a good housewife and prepare tasty everyday meals for my family throughout my life, I was determined that I would find a way to actually enjoy cooking rather than merely being forced to do so as a wife's duty. This was the very beginning of my cooking career. Thirty years have passed since then, and I have widened my career to include the cuisine of not only Japan but also the world. Travel has been a shared pleasure for my family, and we have visited the United States, Europe, Oceania and Asia, which gave me opportunities to learn cooking from a diverse array of the world's chefs and cooking specialists.

Such experiences have helped me in my work, as I have translated foreign cookbooks into Japanese, contributed recipes to numerous

magazines, and written several Japanese-language cookbooks of my own—including two on sushi. I also have been teaching cooking and table decorating in my Art of Dining classes in Tokyo for many years.

The recipes I teach come from both Japan and abroad, and so do my students. In my classes, I find special fulfillment in introducing foreign food to Japanese people, and Japanese food to foreign people. Sharing food is probably the quickest way to get an intimate feel for another culture. It is a direct, sensory experience that helps people develop good feelings toward each other.

It is my hope that my cooking classes, with students of various nationalities, contribute to good grassroots relations between Japan and other countries, and help in some small but concrete way to make the world a better place. In fact, I consider this my life's work.

Another wonderful aspect of cooking is that I'm still learning and improving even after three decades as a culinary professional. No one ever learns everything about the art of food—there is always much more to discover.

And recently, the world has discovered sushi.

Around the 1980s, people in various other countries began enjoying this formal fare in more casual ways. Adapting sushi to local tastes and ingredients led to creative innovations. Some of these, such as the California roll, eventually found their way back to Japan. One reason I wrote this book is to return the favor by sharing Japan's modern sushi with the world. Chefs in Japan create new varieties all the time. There's no need for sushi to be rigidly conservative. Another reason I wrote this book is to help people understand what authentic sushi is like. To use a more widely understood dish to explain my point, Italian culinary experts might be startled to see a teriyaki chicken pizza, but they are likely to accept the idea that this delicious dish is in fact a pizza so long as it respects certain basic rules. For one thing, it would need to have a good crust. Teriyaki chicken sitting on a slice of toast would not count.

Just as a real pizza calls for a real crust, so does real sushi call for real sushi rice. As explained later in this book, it should be firm, glossy, sticky and tangy. The reasons are both aesthetic and practical, but rice with these qualities is one thing that all authentic sushi has in common.

Some of my recipes in this book, especially in the "Global Sushi" section, incorporate ingredients or cooking methods from other cuisines that I have studied around the world. However, I am not a big fan of so-called "borderless" or "fusion" cooking, which often lacks a clear identity. I think the origins of a dish should be identifiable, and that it should express something about the culture in which the food has its roots.

Some of the dishes in this book would look great on the menu of a fine Tokyo restaurant. Others are more like the comfort food a suburban Japanese mother would make for her children. But most of them are new, and all of them are authentic—even those that incorporate touches of other cuisines.

You may be wondering why I haven't mentioned raw fish as a part of authentic sushi. While this is a common sushi ingredient, many types of real Japanese sushi do not include raw fish—or any fish at all. In fact, some popular varieties of sushi are vegetarian-friendly. This book includes a few recipes using raw fish, but many more that do not. Even though I know it to be delicious, I certainly wouldn't force raw fish on anyone who thinks they aren't ready to try it. There are plenty of other wonderful varieties of sushi for you to enjoy.

But after you've tasted a few of them, I think you'll find yourself inspired to try more and more. As you enjoy eating sushi that you have learned to make with your own hands, I hope your reaction will be like mine when I began to explore the cuisines of other cultures. That is, it should seem like a kind of magic.

I would be happy to hear about anything this book has inspired you to create. If you would like to share your discoveries, please feel free to contact me at yumiumemura.com.

SUSHI YESTERDAY AND TODAY

Picture this: One sunny afternoon in Indianapolis, a minivan with a shiny green paint job pulls into the parking lot of a strip mall. The van's side door slides open, and a casually dressed middle-aged woman steps out. Unconsciously reaching up to brush a strand of long blonde hair away from her face, she scans the row of storefronts. She's on her way to watch the auto races for which Indianapolis is famous, but first she wants to get a bite to eat. Her eyes light up as she spots a sushi shop.

Now picture this: One sunny afternoon in the 1830s, some strong-legged men carrying a green palanquin with a shiny coat of lacquer came to a halt near a row of shops in the Ryogoku neighborhood of Edo, the city now called Tokyo. The men set the palanquin down, and one of them slid open a door in its side. A samurai stepped out, unconsciously reaching up to adjust the stylish topknot on his head. He was on his way to watch the sumo matches for which the neighborhood is famous, but first he wanted to get a bite to eat. His eyes lit up as he spotted a sushi shop.

As these two scenes illustrate, sushi has spread far beyond its ancient origins. An exquisite treat for Japan's elite at some points in its history, sushi is now enjoyed by just plain folks across America and around the world. It's a worldwide phenomenon, with sushi catching on from Dublin to Dubai. In Sao Paolo, Brazil, sushi restaurants are now said to outnumber traditional Brazilian barbecue places. And of course there is one more location where sushi will soon be found—your kitchen.

But how did it all begin?

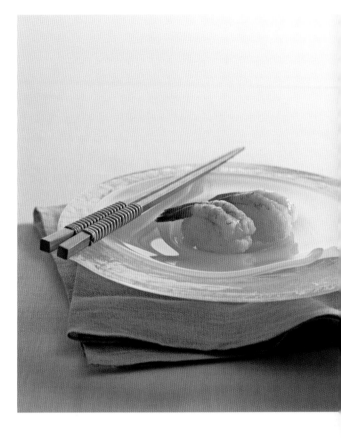

For a food that is now held in such high esteem, sushi has surprisingly humble origins. Like bubble wrap or crumpled newspaper, the rice used in sushi was originally little more than disposable packing material. More than a thousand years ago on the Asian mainland, someone had the idea of storing fish in a sealed jar of cooked rice. The rice would ferment, creating alcohol that prevented the fish from rotting. The fish did change, though, broken down from within by its own enzymes. Fish preserved in this way wound up tasting something like very strong cheese, but it could be safely stored for months. The rice, having absorbed the smellier essences of the aging process, would be thrown away. This primitive proto sushi eventually found its way to Japan.

Around the fifteenth century in Kyoto, which was then Japan's capital, people began letting it age for shorter and shorter periods of time. As a result, the fish became fresher and the rice became more palatable. Eventually, people began eating the rice together with the fish.

From that simple beginning came the wide range of sushi dishes enjoyed today. The most common basic types are maki sushi, in which the rice and other ingredients are rolled up in sheet of nori seaweed, and nigiri sushi, in which a piece of fish or some other morsel is served atop a bite-size portion of rice. Rolled sushi was invented no later than 1776, the year it first appeared in a Japanese cookbook. Nigiri sushi may be even older, but credit for its invention usually goes to Yohei Hanaya, who ran a sushi restaurant Ryogoku, the sumo neighborhood, in the early 1800s.

Other traditional styles include chirashi sushi ("scattered" sushi) and oshi sushi (pressed or molded sushi). Examples of each of these types, and more, appear in this book.

At some points in its long history, sushi has been a casual street food, and at others—including much of the twentieth century—it was a high-class treat. The current era of sushi history has

Sake Decanters and Serving Glasses

Sake and Small Drinking Cups

seen it regain its mass appeal, which has led to an explosion of creative recipes inside Japan and around the world. It can truly be said that we are living in sushi's golden age.

Not only the style of sushi but also its substance has been transformed over the years. For example, salmon was rarely used as a sushi ingredient in Japan as recently as the early 1990s, but now it is very common. This change may have to do with the popularity of salmon—and sushi—in the United States. It was inevitable that American chefs would combine the two, and just as inevitable that the delicious results would spread back to Japan. Similarly, avocado was first used in Los Angeles in the 1960s as a substitute for fresh fatty tuna, which was then hard to find in America. Nowadays, avocado is a respectable sushi ingredient in its own right.

Dramatic sushi innovations have been occurring in Japan, too. Not only are intriguing new types of fish constantly being imported from all around the world, but today's younger Japanese have grown up without the assumption that sushi needs to involve fish at all. At a typical suburban, family-style sushi restaurant in Japan today, you are likely to find sushi topped with beef, pork, poultry or Japanese-style omelet slices. There are even a few popular vegetarian types, such as cucumber rolls or sushi rice stuffed into a sweet inari tofu pouch.

The sushi recipes in this book combine traditional techniques with a modern taste for innovation. As you enjoy making and eating them, you will take your place beside the Indianapolis motor sports fan and the Ryogoku samurai to become a part of sushi history.

SUSHI TOOLS

They say that a craftsman is only as good as his tools, but when it comes to sushi the good news in that only a few tools are absolutely necessary. A superbly supplied Japanese kitchen will include everything shown here, but the only truly indispensable items on this list are makisu bamboo mats and good, sharp knives. Three more items that are nearly as important are a rice tub, a rice paddle and, if you plan to prepare sushi with brown rice, a pressure cooker. A proper tub and paddle make mixing sushi rice a breeze. (They also contribute an enjoyable "traditional" atmosphere to your kitchen.) However, as you will read in the following pages, there are other tools that can serve as practical substitutes. Most of the tools listed in this section should be available at kitchen supply shops or large department stores. Others may be ordered for specialized dealers online. See the Resource Guide on page 156 for hints.

Bamboo
Colander

Bamboo Mat

Bamboo colander (zaru) This handsome item will add as much to your kitchen décor as to your cooking technique. It is a slightly coarse mesh of smooth, narrow bamboo strips held in place by a round or square frame made of wood or more bamboo. The surface is either flat or slightly depressed. In Japan it is often used for making and serving zaru soba, a cool summertime dish of strained noodles served on their colander with a small bowl of dipping sauce on the side. When it comes to sushi, a bamboo colander is useful for cooling thin sheets of freshly cooked egg for the egg-wrapped sushi recipes in Chapter Four.

Bamboo mat (makisu) Based on the ancient design of a bamboo window blind, a rolling mat is essential to making any kind of rolled sushi. Certain elaborate rolls, such as the Flower Rolls on page 62, even require the use of two mats.

The mat is made of bamboo slats woven together with string. If the slats have a flat side and a curved side, use the mat with its flat side up. If the strings are tied off only along one edge of the mat, work with that edge away from you to keep any trailing string ends from getting wrapped up inside your sushi. Be sure your mat is dry when you start to use it, especially when you are making a roll wrapped in nori, which easily becomes soggy.

Chopsticks (hashi) Whether or not to use chopsticks is generally up to you, as etiquette allows most types of sushi to be eaten with your fingers. When setting them out for your guests, however, be aware that chopsticks are set out differently than Western eating utensils. While knives and forks are laid vertically beside the plate, chopsticks are placed horizontally in front of the plate, pointing left. In a formal setting, a chopstick rest is used to keep the tips of the chopsticks from touching the table.

Dish towels (fukin) Keep several of these or other thin cotton cloths nearby to wipe down your knife blade to keep it smooth and effective, and to keep your hands clean. A damp cloth should also be draped over your tub of sushi rice to keep it from drying out in the air and losing its stickiness.

Knives One of the most important tools for sushi-making is a good, sharp knife. Japanese knives, heirs to the nation's proud tradition of sword-smithing, are often of exceptional quality. While it is not strictly necessary to use a specialized Japanese knife, it is imperative to use a very sharp one. A dull knife will never make good sushi. A good knife—frequently wiped clean—is essential to smoothly slicing through fresh fish or cutting rolled sushi into neat, bite-size pieces.

Measuring cup and measuring spoons In this book, 1 cup is 250 milliliters. The volume of cups

Assortment of Sushi Knives

Sushi Molds

Omelet Pan

varies around the world, but 250 milliliters is near enough to standard throughout the West that recipes in this book should work in any Western country. In Japan, however, a cup is just 200 milliliters. If you are using this book in Japan, increase the cup measurements by about ¼. There are also international variations in the size of teaspoons and tablespoons, but these are too slight to make any significant difference in your results.

Molds Almost any container can be used as a mold for sushi rice. If the container is not a nonstick one, be sure to dampen it first, or line it with plastic wrap so that the rice will turn out easily. In Japan, molds with special shapes are used to represent the seasons, with flowers for spring, gourds for autumn and so one.

A traditional wooden boxlike mold is useful for oshi sushi pressed sushi recipes, but any rectangular vessel, from a pound cake pan to a Tupperware box, will do just as well. (Sealable containers such as Tupperware or Rubbermaid products are useful for marinating as well.)

Omelet pan (tamagoyaki-ki) This is a specialized Japanese frying pan notable for its rectangular shape. Thin layers of egg are cooked in it and rolled up to form a bar-shaped omelet. You may use a round skillet for the job instead. In that case, the edges will not be as even, but you can trim these away for a good result.

Pressure cooker This appliance is indispensable for preparing Brown Sushi Rice. Because each grain of brown rice is surrounded by its bran, cooking it under pressure helps force water into the grains to make them soft and sticky. Brown rice cooked without pressure may be too hard and crumbly to make good sushi. If you don't have a pressure cooker, simply substitute white rice.

Rice cooker This is an electrical appliance about the size and shape of a small hatbox, used for cooking rice. Uncooked rice and water are put in a special pot that fits inside the appliance, which boils the water until a sensor detects that the temperature has risen above 212°F (100°C), a sign that all the free water is gone. The appliance then automatically switches over from cooking to warming mode. Zojirushi, a major manufacturer of rice cookers, suggests allowing rice for sushi to "rest" in the warming mode for 15 minutes after it is cooked. However, rice intended for sushi should probably not be left in an active rice cooker for much longer than that, lest it lose too much moisture and become crumbly rather than sticky.

Rice paddles (shamoji) Resembling a large, flattened spoon, this tool allows you to mix cooked rice without crushing the grains. If a standard rice paddle is not available, use another utensil such as a flat spatula, but do not use a curved mixing spoon as this may squish the grains rather than

Rice Paddles

cut between them. When using a wooden shamoji, make sure to wet it so the rice will not stick.

Rice pot To cook rice the low-tech, traditional way, use a tall, heavy-bottomed cooking pot with a tight-fitting lid.

Rice tub (handai or hangiri) This is a round wooden tub, usually made of cypress, used for mixing freshly cooked rice with Sushi Dressing Sauce. Its broad shape helps you mix the rice without crushing the grains, and also helps the rice to cool evenly as you fan it. Moreover, the wood helps to soak up excess moisture.

Ideally, the tub should be soaked in water and wiped dry before each use. (This keeps the thirsty wood from soaking up too much moisture too soon.) Afterward, rinse it thoroughly—do not use soap—and store it upside down in a cool, dry place. If you don't have a traditional rice tub, substitute any large, wide-bottomed container, ideally an unwaxed salad bowl. A plastic or stainless steel container will also do, although these materials will not absorb excess moisture.

Sesame roaster Roasting sesame seeds helps to bring out their flavor. A sesame roaster is a merely small pan

Sesame Seed Roaster

with an attachable screen lid. You simply put the seeds in the pan, close the lid, and cook them over very low heat until they begin to pop and jump around. You can also use a regular small frying pan with a screen splatter guard.

Sushi platter (oke) This is a lacquered serving platter specially designed for serving sushi. With its flat bottom and high rim, it shares its basic shape with a rice tub, but is far more ornate and elegant. A sushi oke is definitely meant for presenting sushi, but not for preparing it.

Uchiwa (fan) This traditional round fan is very handy for cooling hot rice while you mix in the Sushi Dressing Sauce, but a stiff piece of cardboard or even an electric fan turned to its gentlest setting will do the trick as well. Old-fashioned uchiwa fans were made of decorated paper pasted onto a framework of bamboo ribs, but nowadays the bamboo has generally been supplanted by plastic.

Wasabi grater The traditional way to grate a wasabi root into paste is by rubbing it against a patch of naturally abrasive sharkskin attached to a small wooden paddle. But if you don't have this deluxe item already on hand, any vegetable grater capable of fine work will do.

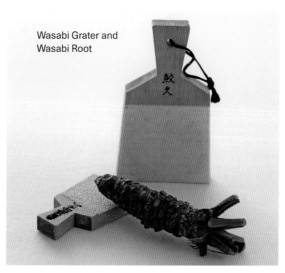
Wasabi Grater and Wasabi Root

SUSHI INGREDIENTS

Many of the ingredients listed here are increasingly widely available at ordinary supermarkets, and most of the rest should be in stock at your nearest Asian or gourmet food store. But if you can't find them locally, there are online merchants who carry them (see the Resource Guide).

Clockwise from the top:
Mitsuba, Ginger, Shiso,
Myoga Buds, Wasabi Root

Bamboo shoots (takenoko) In its natural state, this crunchy vegetable resembles a cone-shaped flower bud that may be the size of your fist or significantly larger. It is wrapped in tough outer leaves and takes some work to prepare. Bamboo shoots are also available peeled, sliced and canned or packed in water. For the sake of simplicity, this book calls for the commercially prepared variety.

Bonito (katsuo) This fish, a smaller relative of the tuna, has a firm red flesh that is delicious when eaten fresh. Bonito meat is also dried and shaved into paper-thin **bonito flakes (katsuo bushi)** that are used as a condiment and boiled to make dashi broth.

Crab sticks (kanikama) For convenience, some of the recipes in this book call for imitation crab sticks, as they are easy to obtain, come in a uniform size, and are widely consumed in Japan. Of course, you may always use fresh crabmeat if you wish.

Dashi stock A clear broth that is basic to Japanese cooking, the most representative dashi may be made at home with bonito flakes and kombu seaweed. Instant dashi, usually sold in powdered form, is also widely available.

Denbu Moist, flaky fish that might be described as "scrambled fish" or "scrambled shrimp," denbu is used like a condiment to add a touch of color and flavor to various sushi dishes. You may find it in the refrigerator section of an Asian market, but there is also a recipe for making your own on page 58.

Edamame A healthy Japanese snack whose popularity has recently gone worldwide, edamame are young green soybeans quickly boiled and then served in their pods, often with a sprinkling of salt. The name literally means "branch beans," as fresh edamame sometimes come in

Edamame

bunches of pods still attached to their branch. By the time they reach the supermarket's produce section, however, the branches have usually been removed. Bags of precooked edamame may also be found in the frozen foods section. Edamame are casual finger food, and the normal way to eat them is to squeeze the beans out of their pods with your fingers.

Eel (unagi) The fresh-water eel called "unagi" is enjoyed year-round in Japan, but especially in the summer, when eating it is said to make hot weather more bearable. This fish has a sweet, succulent, fatty flesh that is almost always prepared kabayaki-style, filleted and broiled with sweet soy glaze. Being cooked, unagi is a good choice for people who do not like raw fish. Unagi is sometimes confused with anago, or conger eel, a sea-dwelling creature whose firmer, drier flesh has charms of its own, but which is not used in this book.

If you live in Britain, unagi should be readily available at your local fishmonger. Residents of North America may have to look a bit harder, but it can be found at Asian or gourmet groceries and may be ordered frozen from online dealers.

Fish cakes (hanpen) This fluffy white fish cake, with a firm yet spongy consistency, may be found in the refrigerated section of an Asian grocery store.

Fried tofu (abura-age) These thin slabs of fried tofu can be sweetened, cut in half and opened out to make the little pouches that are the defining ingredient for various kinds of inari sushi. They should be purchased already fried at an Asian grocer or from an online specialty retailer. If you are lucky you may find fresh ones, but abura-age are usually sold in a plastic pouch that may or may not contain a dark broth. The type with the broth are pre-sweetened, but their ingredients and flavor can be unpredictable. For that reason, the recipes in this book call for the plain type, which you can turn into sweet Tofu Sushi Pouches on your own by following the recipe on page 38.

Ginger This knobbly root is not the world's most photogenic vegetable, as it often resembles a handful of small, misshapen potatoes fused together. But sharp, powerful flavors await inside. Those flavors can be released by grating or mincing the hard, fibrous flesh to use as an ingredient in a sauce, or by slicing it up into thin discs to boil or stir-fry with other ingredients.

Japanese cucumbers (kyuri) Japanese cucumbers, called kyuri, are slender and nearly seedless. Their skin is a deep, uniform green, without the pale areas that may be seen on fatter cucumber varieties. They are ideally suited for slicing into ribbonlike strips or small, coin-shaped discs.

Japanese leeks (naganegi) Sometimes called a "long onion," this vegetable differs from Western leeks in two key respects. One is that a Japanese leek is only about half as thick as a regular leek. The more important difference is that a leek's skin is very stiff and tough when uncooked, whereas a naganegi is tender throughout. However, a leek will soften when cooked, which

makes it a useful substitute in the Sukiyaki Sushi recipe, in which the major ingredients are thoroughly sautéed. Leeks should be sliced more thinly than naganegi to ensure that they cook fully.

Kelp (kombu) This tough, broad-leafed seaweed is used to make dashi broth and to give flavor to rice. It is usually sold in large, dark, dried pieces.

Lotus root (renkon) This delightfully crunchy vegetable has a mild flavor but an exciting shape. In its raw form, it looks like a string of fat sausage links, and when you cut any of the links in half you will find a semi-hollow cross-section that resembles a wagon wheel, or a cathedral's rose window. Lotus roots should be peeled before you use them, and soaking them in water with a little vinegar will preserve their white color.

Mirin This sweet, low-alcohol rice wine is used mainly for cooking. It should be easy to find in a supermarket near the oils, vinegars or imported condiments, but sweet cooking sherry will do as a substitute in a pinch.

Miso This fermented soybean paste is used in countless Japanese recipes. The simplest of them is plain miso soup, made by dissolving a heaping spoonful of it in a bowl of hot dashi. A hot bowl of miso soup is an excellent finish to a sushi meal.

Miso has the consistency of peanut butter but is far less sticky. Rich in protein and vitamin B, miso comes in colors ranging from golden yellow to reddish brown to nearly black, with the darker varieties tending to have stronger flavor. The type to use is up to you. Miso can be found in the seasonings or refrigerated section of your supermarket.

Mitsuba This aromatic Japanese herb, also known as "trefoil" or "Japanese parsley," has tender leaves on very long stems. The stems can be used as edible strings to tie little bundles of sushi together, but spring onions (or slender green onions/scallions) may be substituted for this purpose. Whether you're using mitsuba stems or green onions, wilt them in a quick bath of boiling water to make them easier to work with.

Myoga ginger buds This plant is a member of the ginger family, but while ordinary ginger concentrates flavor in its roots, the sharp taste of myoga is found in its large, reddish, tightly furled buds. Shredded or very thinly sliced myoga buds can be used as a piquant garnish.

Nori seaweed A type of dried and flavored seaweed that is essential to a great many sushi recipes, nori is most commonly sold in paperlike sheets that are about 7 x 8 inches (18 x 20 cm) in size. Nori should be crisp, yet flexible.

If you live in a humid climate, you may find that nori easily becomes soggy after its package has been open for a while. If this happens, simply wave each sheet of wilted nori over a gas flame for a moment or two to revive it, or dry it briefly in a toaster oven.

Oyster mushroom (eringi) This big, thick mushroom is almost all stem, topped by a small, flat cap. Its pale flesh takes well to sautees, especially in butter, but it is also large enough to be sliced up

Pickled Ginger

and grilled. In English, it is also known as a king oyster mushroom, king trumpet mushroom or royal trumpet mushroom.

Pickled ginger (gari) Paperlike slices of pale pink pickled ginger, called "gari" in sushi chef jargon, are commonly offered as a palate-cleanser between sushi servings. The best way to serve it is to place a small dish on the table and let your guests help themselves to a little bite now and then. This type of pickle is made with new ginger, which is tender and fragrant.

For sushi purposes, avoid beni-shoga, a type of shredded pickled ginger that is dyed bright red and is used as a condiment for non sushi Japanese dishes such as gyodon beef bowls and yakisoba grilled noodles.

Potato starch (katakuriko) This starch is used as a thickening agent in Japan. Cornstarch is its functional equivalent and a good substitute.

Red pepper powder (ichimi togarashi) This is Japanese red pepper, used as a condiment. Cayenne pepper is a good substitute.

Rice vinegar (su) Rice vinegar is the traditional active ingredient for turning plain rice into sushi rice, but some recipes in this book also call for wine vinegar or raspberry vinegar for varied flavor. If a particular type of vinegar isn't specified in a recipe, rice vinegar is the preferred choice. How-

Nori Seaweed

Essential Flavoring and Seasoning Agents for Making Sushi: Vinegars, Soy Sauce, Salt, Citrus, Sake and Shichimi Togarashi

Sea Bream (Tai)

ever, another mild vinegar, sush as white or cider vinegar can also be used.

Sake Japan's national alcoholic drink, sake should be easy to find at any liquor retailer. It is often described as "rice wine." Both sweet and dry varieties exist, and the type you choose to drink depends on your taste.

For Japanese cooking, however, dry sake should be used to bring out the flavor of the ingredients.

Salmon (sake) The Japanese word for salmon is "sake." To avoid confusion with the drink, this is sometimes pronounced "shake." Salmon may be eaten fresh, smoked or cooked, but salmon that is eaten raw should first have been deep-frozen. The reason is that salmon are susceptible to parasites that could harm humans. However, this risk can be eliminated by cooking or deep-freezing, which kills the parasites.

Salt (shio) Ordinary table salt is well-suited to Sushi Dressing Sauce and other recipes in this book, but for a little extra flavor you may wish to use sea salt or rock salt. However, if you choose a coarse salt for your Sushi Dressing Sauce, be sure to grind it first to make sure that it fully dissolves.

Sansho pepper Also known as Szechuan pepper, sansho has only a mildly spicy flavor but also creates an intriguing tingly sensation in the mouth. Sansho powder is a popular condiment for grilled eel, and tiny sansho leaves are sometimes used as a garnish.

Sea bream (tai) This white-meat fish is a symbol of good luck in Japan. The lucky god Ebisu is usually portrayed as a fisherman who has just caught one, and a large bream is a traditional—if now rather old-fashioned—gift for happy occasions. When uncooked, bream has a "fishier"

White and Black Sesame Seeds

Dried Shiitake Mushrooms

flavor than darker-fleshed fishes such as tuna. To moderate this taste, you may want to marinate the bream for a few minutes in a mixture of lemon juice and olive oil with a light sprinkling of pepper and salt. If bream is unavailable in your supermarket, try another white-meat fish, such as yellowtail, sole, horse mackerel or sea bass. Pickled herring is another good substitute as it comes already marinated, but be sure to choose the simplest variety, without any additional flavorings such as cream sauce or dill.

Sesame oil (goma abura) Made from roasted sesame seeds, this oil has a strong, rich, smoky flavor and is often used for seasoning foods.

Sesame seeds (goma) These seeds come in black, white and gold varieties, and should be toasted for maximum flavor and ease of digestion. Read the label carefully, as some varieties come already toasted.

Shiitake mushroom Over the past 20 or 30 years, this dark, meaty mushroom with a distinctive earthy flavor has become popular worldwide, and it is now cultivated in countries to which it is

not native, such as the United States and China. Shiitakes are sold in both dry and fresh form, with the dried mushrooms being preferable. Not only does the drying and aging amplify their flavor, but some research has suggested that sun-dried mushrooms may be an excellent source of vitamin D. Dried shiitakes should be allowed to soak in water for at least an hour (preferably overnight) to soften up before cooking.

Note that the water in which they have soaked becomes very flavorful and is often used as a recipe ingredient.

Shirataki noodles These pale, almost translucent noodles are normally made from a Japanese root vegetable called konnyaku, although some varieties now on the market include tofu as an ingredient. These very chewy noodles are a key element in dishes such as sukiyaki. They are sold packed in water, usually in a plastic bag, and may be found in the refrigerated section of your supermarket.

Shiso leaf Also known in English as "perilla" (and less commonly as "beefsteak plant" or "oba"), shiso is a green leaf of a rounded teardrop shape

Clockwise from the top: Abura-age Fried Tofu, Shimeji Mushrooms, Japanese Cucumbers, Eringi Mushrooms, Spring Onions, Young Ginger, Myoga, Wasabi Root, Yuzu, Lemon, Dried Kombu Seaweed

with frilly edges. It may grow as large as the palm of your hand. It has a distinctive flavor marked by notes of basil and mint.

In Japan, whole fresh shiso leaves are commonly used to garnish sashimi. They are also sometimes coated with batter on one side and fried as tempura. Shredded shiso leaves may be tossed into salads, while pureed shiso leaves add flavor to Japanese salad dressings and even beverages. For the recipes in this book, fresh basil is a useful substitute.

Shrimp (ebi) In recipes in this book calling for cooked shrimp, any shrimp of an appropriate size will do. Certain recipes call for "ama-ebi," or sweet shrimp, which can be eaten raw. Ama-ebi are pale and slender, each a little thicker than a pencil.

Soy sauce (shoyu) This basic Japanese condiment, brewed from soybeans, wheat and salt, comes in two major varieties: ordinary and light. The light soy sauce has a higher salt content. Its paler color makes it valuable to use when cooking with foods that have attractive colors of their own.

Spring onion Pencil-thin, and often much thinner, these tender young onions are also known as green onions and scallions. The type usually found in Japan tend to be almost perfectly straight, with virtually no bulb at the white end. Both the green and white parts are edible, and are usually chopped into small pieces. (*See also* Japanese Leeks.)

Sugar (sato) Ordinary table sugar may be used to make Sushi Dressing Sauce. It is easier to use a more finely ground sugar, as this dissolves more quickly. But whatever kind of sugar you use, make sure that it is pure. This means confectioner's sugar should be avoided, as it usually contains cornstarch or other additives that can lead to un sushi-like results.

Sushi rice This is the key to good sushi. Use a California short-grain rice, or a Japanese short-grain rice such as Koshihikari. The rice may be white or brown, although brown rice should be prepared in a pressure cooker to achieve optimal sushi tenderness. Do not use long-grain rice or instant rice of any kind.

Tofu This versatile soy-based food can be prepared in countless ways. Plain tofu is generally

Fresh Tofu

Wasabi

either firm or soft, and either kind can be eaten cooked or fresh. Firm tofu holds up better to cooking, however, which is why it is called for in the Tofu Sushi recipe on page 45.

Wasabi Sometimes compared to horseradish, wasabi is a plant that grows in Japan along mountain streams. Its root, shaped like a small, knobby carrot, is ground or grated to make a green paste with a fiery flavor that will affect diners' sinuses as much as their tongues. Most cooks in Japan take advantage of ready-to-use wasabi paste (often artificially flavored) that is sold in tubes or jars and is now available in much of the world.

Although it is a very popular item that is essential for many kinds of sushi, its high-octane spiciness can come as a surprise to the uninitiated. Use wasabi sparingly at first, and then use more as you come to like it.

Yuzu This small, aromatic citrus fruit is not eaten by itself, but its juice and zest are popular flavorings in Japanese cooking. Its scent is so clean and refreshing that not only is it used in recipes, but people sometimes set several yuzu afloat in a steaming bathtub to create a luxurious scented bath. If your grocer doesn't stock it, substitute lemon.

SUSHI BASICS

Sushi rice is special. As the literal foundation of most sushi recipes, the rice must stick together well enough to support the other ingredients. It needs to have a clean, appealing taste of its own without distracting from the other flavors that make sushi such a joy to eat. And it must be pleasing to look at, meaning that it is white and shiny and composed of clearly defined individual grains. The sushi rice recipes that follow will guide you through the process of making perfect sushi rice every time. Properly made sushi rice is not difficult to achieve; it simply takes care and attention.

Once you've made sushi rice, be sure to read "Sushi Tips" (pages 26–29) before trying one of the recipes. If you're a beginner at making sushi, these tips will help you avoid typical sushi making pitfalls—such as rice that's become too dry to work with.

Yet the most important sushi-making tip I can give you is to urge you to be versatile and to have fun. At a basic level, this means that recipes in this book that call for brown rice can also be made with white rice, and vice-versa. And in many cases, unavailable ingredients may be eliminated, especially when you are making sushi rolls with several fillings. Don't be afraid to improvise substitutions for other ingredients when necessary. You may discover something wonderful.

Be inventive. Think of your favorite food combinations that are popular in your own culture to create your own sushi recipes. I hope that you use this book as a jumping-off point to explore your own creativity. It's the best tip of all!

Basic Sushi Rice

For practical and aesthetic reasons, including pleasing our taste buds, sushi rice is firm, glossy, sticky and tangy. Some of the recipes in this book include innovative shortcuts for creating easy versions of sushi rice, using "Simple White Rice" as the base with handy ingredients such as lemon or lime juice to give the rice its requisite mildly sweet tang. But the traditional kind, using rice vinegar-based Sushi Dressing Sauce, can be used in all of the recipes in this book. Here's how to make sushi rice the old fashioned way on the stovetop.

Time 1 hour
Makes 1 standard quantity (about 2½ cups/400 g)

1 cup (200 g) uncooked Japanese or California
    short-grain rice
1 cup (250 ml) water
1 teaspoon sake (optional)
1 piece of kombu dried kelp, a few inches square
    (optional)

SUSHI DRESSING SAUCE
5 teaspoons rice vinegar
2 teaspoons sugar
1½ teaspoons salt

Thoroughly rinse the rice in several changes of water until it runs crystal clear. Soak the rice in water for at least 30 minutes and drain thoroughly before cooking.

Bring the water to a boil in a saucepan, adding the sake if desired. Drain the rice and add it to the boiling water. Stir once, and return to a boil. Add the kombu, if using. Reduce the heat to the lowest setting, cook for 10 minutes, then turn off the heat and allow it to stand for 5–10 minutes more, covered, to finish cooking. (Note: Although this stovetop method is my preferred way to prepare sushi rice, you may also use an automatic rice cooker. If you're using a rice cooker, use the same amounts described above and follow the manufacturer's instructions.)

1 Rinsed short-grain rice ready to be drained	**2** Rice cooked with kombu	**3** Cooked rice ready for mixing	**4** Adding Sushi Dressing Sauce to cooked rice	**5** Mixing rice with Sushi Dressing Sauce in the handai

To make the Sushi Dressing Sauce, combine the vinegar, sugar and salt in a cup, and mix well until the sugar and salt are fully dissolved. The sauce should become clear. Remove the kombu and turn the rice into a large wooden mixing bowl or handai. If you have no wooden containers, a non-reactive casserole dish or deep platter will suffice.

Avoid digging or scooping the rice out of the saucepan, as this will damage some of the grains. It helps, however, to run a rice paddle or spatula around the edges of the cooked rice to loosen it before turning it out of the saucepan. Once it is in the bowl, gently break up the mass of rice with a few smooth, straight, slicing motions of your spatula. Pour the Sushi Dressing Sauce slowly over the back of your rice paddle or spatula, moving it to and fro over the rice so that the sauce is evenly sprinkled all over the rice.

Mix the rice to distribute the sauce thoroughly. To preserve the integrity of the grains and avoid mashing them together, do not use circular stirring motions but instead "slice" the rice at an angle with your paddle or spatula, lifting it and turning it over in sections or chunks.

When the sauce is well distributed, begin to fan the rice while continuing to mix it. (You can do this yourself, but it's much easier to have a helper do the fanning while you do the mixing.) Fanning will cool the rice to a usable temperature and also helps evaporate the excess moisture. The sugar will give the grains an appealing gloss, which is an essential characteristic of good sushi rice.

Moisten and wring out a fine cotton cloth such as a thin dish towel or cloth napkin and place it on top of the rice to keep it from drying out. The cloth should rest lightly on the surface of the rice. Keep it covered until you are ready to make sushi with it. Rice covered in this way should remain good for several hours, or until the cloth dries out. Remoisten the cloth if it dries out.

Sushi rice will loose some flavor if kept out for more than a few hours. Leftover sushi rice can be refrigerated or frozen and later warmed up with steam or in a microwave, but it will lose some flavor and stickiness in the process.

For best results, eat it all on the day you make it.

Note: This recipe may be doubled or even tripled, but it should not be reduced.

Brown Sushi Rice

Although white rice is a staple in Japan, brown rice—called "genmai"—is enjoyed as well. Some of the recipes in this book take advantage of genmai's darker color and extra flavor by using it instead of white rice as the basis of sushi. Brown rice tends to be harder and less sticky than the white variety, but this method gives you rice that is easy to work with and that has a classic sushi mouthfeel.

To make Brown Sushi Rice, use a brown variety of Japanese or California short-grain rice and follow the same recipe as for Basic Sushi Rice—but with some key differences. Soak the rice for at least 1 hour instead of 30 minutes and instead of cooking the rice in an ordinary pot or rice cooker, use a pressure cooker, following the instructions that came with your particular model.

Time 1 hour
Makes 1 standard quantity (about 2½ cups/400 g)

1 cup (about 200 g) uncooked brown short-grain rice
1¼ cups plus 1 tablespoon (325 ml) hot water
⅛ teaspoon salt
1 quantity Sushi Dressing Sauce (page 23)

Rinse, soak and drain the brown rice according to the directions for Basic Sushi Rice, but soak the rice for 1 to 2 hours rather than 30 minutes. Then, combine the rice with the hot water and salt in a pressure cooker, cover and bring to a boil. When the pressure indicator rises and steam begins to come out, reduce the heat to low and cook for 20 minutes. Finally, turn off the heat and let the pressure cooker stand until the indicator shows that it is safe to open.

Once the rice is cooked, prepare it as sushi rice using the Sushi Dressing Sauce.

Simple White Rice

Basic Sushi Rice has a mild sweetness and subtle tang, thanks to the sugar and vinegar in the Sushi Dressing Sauce. In some recipes in this book, however, other ingredients will provide those same qualities. When a recipe calls for Simple White Rice, follow the same steps as you would in making Basic Sushi Rice, but omit the Sushi Dressing Sauce.

Time 45 minutes
Makes 1 standard quantity (about 2 cups/400 g)

Pickled New Ginger

Pickled Ginger (Gari)

This recipe can be made with ordinary ginger, though new ginger is preferred because it is less fibrous, which makes it easier to cut—and chew. New ginger is paler and milder than ordinary ginger.

Time 15 minutes plus at least 30 minutes for marinating
Makes about 1 cup (110 g)

3½ oz (100 g) fresh ginger, peeled,
**   or fresh new ginger, unpeeled**
6 tablespoons rice vinegar
4 tablespoons sugar
1 teaspoon salt

Slice the ginger very thin. Spread the ginger slices on a wire rack and pour boiling water over them. This should make them pale and softer, and it will mellow their flavor. Prepare a marinade by mixing the rice vinegar, sugar and salt. Soak the ginger slices in the marinade for at least for 30 minutes.

SUSHI TIPS

PURCHASE FRESH FISH AND SEAFOOD

Unless otherwise specified, the fish used in this book's recipes should be raw—and that means it has to be not just fresh, but super-fresh. But how can you tell? Asking the person behind the fish counter for help in selecting "sashimi grade" fish is a good place to start. Be aware, however, that at least in the United States there is no official government definition of what "sashimi grade" is. Use your own judgment, in addition to the fishmonger's advice, keeping the following guidelines in mind.

When buying whole fish, start by looking them in the eye. The eyes of a fresh fish should be clean and clear, not cloudy, and they should appear rounded and plump, not sunken. The gills should be moist and bright pink or red, not dry and dark. The color of the skin or scales should also be bright, clean and shiny. When you touch the fish, it should feel firm. Finally, have a sniff.

If the fish smells faintly like the ocean, that's a good sign.

But if the fish smells "fishy," throw it back and pick another. Once you have found your fish, ask the fishmonger to dress it for you. Let him or her know that you would prefer long, relatively narrow fillets that you can easily slice into standard sashimi pieces at home.

When buying fillets, look for an even, attractive color. Avoid pieces with any obvious discoloration, especially darkening near the edges. Again, touching the fish should reveal its flesh to be firm and resilient, not spongy, sticky, stiff or mushy. If the fish is sold in a tray, make sure there is no liquid accumulating in the bottom of it, as fish that is weeping liquid is not fresh enough to eat raw. Unless the fish is sealed in plastic, apply the same sniff test as for whole fish. (If you can smell it through the plastic, don't even think about buying it.)

When buying frozen fish, understand that modern technology has blurred the line between fresh and frozen. Powerful flash freezers at processing plants and aboard large fishing vessels are now used to preserve fish at a level of freshness that ordinary freezing can't touch. Flash freezing also kills parasites that are sometimes found in certain fish— especially salmon, which should not be eaten raw unless it has previously been flash-frozen. Flash-frozen fish should appear to be almost in a state of suspended animation. It should not be encrusted with ice crystals and it should have no visible traces of dryness or freezer burn. Used immediately after thawing out in your refrigerator, flash-frozen fish is virtually indistinguishable from the conventionally fresh kind. Your own kitchen freezer is no match for an industrial flash freezer, so do not try freezing fresh fish for sushi yourself, and never refreeze fish under any circumstances.

When it comes to shrimp, frozen ones are fine for the recipes in this book that call for shrimp to be cooked. In the case of ama-ebi sweet shrimp, which are often eaten raw, look for shrimp that still have their shells on—and their heads, too, as headless shrimp tend to dry out more quickly. The flesh should be extremely light in color, even to the point of near translucence, with no discoloration or blotchiness. As with fish, if it has an odor that is even slightly unpleasant, don't buy it.

Finally, remember that raw seafood is perishable. Put it in your refrigerator as soon as you get it home, and don't buy it until you are ready to use it—preferably the same day.

KEEP YOUR RICE MOIST

Sushi rice must be moist to work with, but it dries out very easily. Once the rice has been prepared, drape a thin, moist cloth over the rice tub to prevent moisture from escaping.

SLICE YOUR FISH CLEANLY

Sashimi is very fresh fish eaten on its own or used as a sushi topping. It is usually served in small, rectangular slices that are diagonally cut from a larger fillet. If you were cutting a stick of butter, your knife would move in a downward path perpendicular to the tabletop. When slicing sashimi, however, your knife should move downward through the fish in a path that is diagonal to

the tabletop. If you are right-handed, begin working from the end of the fillet that is on your left. Use the fingers of your left hand to carefully hold the fish in place on the board. To properly grasp the knife, place one finger of your right hand along the top (non-sharp side) of the blade, pointing toward the tip, as a guide. This will give you a much better feel for the blade's position than simply wrapping your fist around the hilt.

Cut at enough of an angle (downward and to the left) to give yourself a thin, rectangular slice of fish measuring about 1¼ x 2½ inches (3 x 6 cm). To approximate these dimensions, simply aim for two finger-widths x four finger-widths. The thickness of each slice is up to you, but don't go much above ½ inch (1 cm).

As for your slicing motion, don't saw through the fish as you might with a finished sushi roll or a loaf of bread. Don't even press the knife down as you would with a stick of butter. Instead, begin with the near end of the blade (the part closest to the handle) resting against the near edge of the fish, with the tip of the knife pointing upward and away from you. Then, pull the knife down and toward you, lowering the tip as you go so that the blade slides through the fish and down to the cutting board in one smooth, continuous motion.

AVOID STICKY FINGERS

Sushi rice is very sticky, and your fingers can get sticky working on it. Keep a bowl of water nearby to dip your fingers in from time to time, and a cloth handy to wipe them.

(Of course, your fingers shouldn't be soaking wet, or your rice may become soggy.) Ideally, the water should have a little vinegar in it.

TUCK IN YOUR ROLL

When making a roll, especially a thick one, use the fingers of one hand to push in any loose contents at the end of the roll while holding the bamboo mat firmly around the roll with your other hand.

SLICE YOUR ROLLS CLEANLY

When slicing a roll, wipe the blade with a damp cloth between each slice. Otherwise, minuscule bits of rice adhering to the blade from one slice will make the next slice less neat. Also, it is easier to cut a roll if it is covered in plastic wrap. Drape a piece of wrap over the roll and use the fingers of one hand to hold the wrap firmly against the cutting board while using a knife to slice through the roll with a sawing motion. If you used plastic while rolling the roll, remove that sheet and drape it or a fresh one over the roll. If you start cutting when the plastic is completely wrapped around the roll, the plastic will be more difficult to remove.

ANCHOR YOUR CUTTING BOARD

To keep your cutting board steady, set it on top of a damp folded towel. This will keep it from sliding on your counter or table, and help you to cut neatly.

CHAPTER ONE

NIGIRI AND OTHER BITE-SIZE SUSHI

Variety is one of the many keys to sushi's popularity. Whether you are inquiring about the chef's specialties at a high-class sushi bar, watching a never-ending conveyor belt parade of sushi at a more downscale establishment, or admiring a colorful sushi platter at a home party, taking a moment to choose your next bite is one of sushi's initial pleasures. Of course, you'll want to have more than just one bite in any of those situations, so it helps if each serving is small. This chapter focuses on three basic types of sushi that are both delicious and dainty. Nigiri sushi is the best known of the three. If you asked the average person to draw a picture of a piece of sushi, they would probably sketch a piece of nigiri sushi, which is basically a slice of fish atop a serving of rice small enough to fit in the palm of your hand. The name literally means "squeezed sushi," and it fits in your hand because that is where it is traditionally made.

The range of possible toppings for nigiri sushi is virtually endless. Bright red, lean tuna is the classic choice, but in modern times it has been overtaken in popularity by tuna toro, which is a paler, softer, fattier cut of the same fish. Plenty of other fish varieties are also used, along with modern ingredients ranging from asparagus to duck.

Making nigiri sushi takes some skill, but basic proficiency can be acquired with a little practice. You may have seen sushi chefs slap together perfectly formed pieces of nigiri sushi with dramatic gestures and lightning speed, but the show-manship is optional. Feel free to proceed slowly and deliberately at home. You'll soon get the hang of it. Ball sushi, the second type presented in this chapter, is less traditional but offers a handy shortcut to turning out ready-to-serve sushi quickly and easily. Sushi rice and toppings are combined on a sheet of plastic wrap, and the wrap is then twisted tight to press the ingredients into a tasty little ball.

Sushi canapés are the third category of petite sushi. They use a small portion of sushi rice as the pedestal upon which you can artfully arrange a variety of ingredients. The recipes here call for eye-catching and palate-pleasing combinations such as mango and mint, making these a good introductory sushi for your guests who may not (yet) have discovered the joys of raw fish.

Tuna Nigiri Sushi   Shrimp Nigiri Sushi   Salmon Nigiri Sushi

NIGIRI SUSHI BASICS

Each piece of nigiri sushi calls for about ½ ounce (15 grams), or 1½ tablespoons, of rice. An easy way to do this measurement by eye is to simply aim for a clump of rice about the same size and shape as a wine cork. One standard quantity Basic Sushi Rice (page 23) will yield about 24 pieces of nigiri sushi, which is sufficient for all of the nigiri sushi recipes in this chapter.

Professional sushi chefs can reach into a tub of sushi rice and deftly create a cork-shaped nigiri rice ball one-handed the very moment they intend to use it. But an acceptable shortcut for home cooks is to make a large number of such rice balls a few minutes in advance, arrange them on a plate, and keep them covered with a damp cloth so they do not dry out until you are ready to use them. You may even choose to shape your rice in one of the nigiri sushi molds that are now commercially available. You should know the traditional way, but as a practical matter feel free to use the method that works best for you.

For right-handed sushi chefs, the traditional technique is to place a rectangular slice of sashimi (fresh fish) in your left hand, resting it where your palm and base of your fingers meet. With your right hand, take a cork-sized quantity of rice from your rice tub and roll it between your fingers and palm to form an oblong shape. (Remember that slightly wet hands will help keep the rice from sticking to your skin.) Then, while still holding the rice in your right palm, scoop up a dab of wasabi paste, about ⅛ teaspoon, with your right forefinger and spread it on the fish in your left hand.

Place the rice on top of the fish, and curve your left hand around it so that your palm and fingers form "walls" to hold everything in place. Extend the first two fingers of your right hand, and use them to make a "lid" over the rice, gently patting the rice to firm it up and help it stick to the fish. Next, push in the ends of the oblong piece of rice to neaten. Finally, turn the finished nigiri sushi out of your left hand and onto a serving plate, with the fish side up.

Nigiri sushi is usually served with a small, very shallow dish of plain soy sauce for guests to dip a corner of the sushi into if they wish. Many people, even in Japan, lightly touch the rice side of their nigiri sushi in the soy sauce. However, proper Japanese etiquette requires that you turn or tilt each piece of nigiri sushi when dipping it so that the fish (or other topping), and not the rice, is what touches the sauce. However you do it, keep in mind that the soy sauce is optional, and that the merest trace of it will suffice. Sushi should never be soaked in soy sauce.

Sea Bream Nigiri Sushi

Tuna Toro Sushi

TRADITIONAL NIGIRI SUSHI

This assortment of today's most popular raw seafood sushi toppings puts an attractive range of colors on your serving plate, from white (tai sea bream) through various shades of pink (tuna toro and salmon) to deep red (tuna). As for the petite sweet-fleshed ama-ebi shrimp, they border on translucent.

Time 20 minutes plus 1 hour for rice and ingredient preparation
Makes 20 pieces

4 sashimi slices of tuna (about 3 oz/80 g total)
4 sashimi slices of tuna toro (about 3 oz/80 g total)
4 sashimi slices of tai sea bream or red snapper (about 3 oz/80 g total)
4 sashimi slices of salmon (about 3 oz/80 g total)
8 fresh ama-ebi shrimp or other very small fresh shrimp or 4 medium-size boiled shrimp
20 nigiri rice balls
1 tablespoon wasabi paste
2 or 3 chives, cut into thin 2-in (5-cm)-long strips
Soy sauce for dipping

❶ Prepare the sashimi slices according to the instructions in "Sushi Tips" on pages 28–29.

❷ Remove heads from the ama-ebi shrimp. Shell the shrimp, rinse them and pat them dry. If you're using medium-size shrimp, shell and devein them and then boil them until just done. Cut the shrimp lengthwise down the middle of its belly side, but do not cut through the shrimp.

❸ Prepare the nigiri rice balls according to the instructions in "Nigiri Sushi Basics," opposite. Pair each slice of tuna with one nigiri rice ball according to the same instructions. Repeat for the tuna toro, sea bream and salmon. Garnish the salmon with the chives.

❹ For the shrimp nigiri sushi, lay two of the slender ama-ebi shrimp side by side on your palm, belly-up. If you're using medium-size shrimp, place one shrimp, belly-up, on your palm. Open the shrimp like a book. Dab the shrimp lightly with wasabi and then place one nigiri rice ball on top of the shrimp. Follow the remaining instructions in "Nigiri Sushi Basics" and turn out onto a plate. Repeat with the remaining shrimp for a total of four pieces of shrimp nigiri sushi, each with two little shrimp or one medium-size shrimp on top.

QUICK-AND-EASY SUSHI BITES

These petite balls of sushi make an ideal party snack because you can pop them in your mouth without missing a beat in the conversation. The recipe presented here produces a variety platter featuring shrimp, tuna, salmon and scrambled eggs. You can customize the recipe by substituting tiny slices of pickled herring, fresh yellowtail, or any other favorite sushi topping. By the same token, if you are crazy about shrimp (or any other flavor here), just increase that ingredient and eliminate the others.

Time 30 minutes plus 1 hour for rice preparation
Makes about 16 bite-size sushi balls

1 quantity Basic Sushi Rice (page 23)
2 fresh medium shrimp
1 tablespoon sake (optional)
1 egg
½ tablespoon mirin
1 tablespoon sugar
Pinch of salt
2 teaspoons wasabi paste
4 bite-size pieces, about 1¼-in (3-cm) square, of fresh tuna
4 bite-size pieces, about 1¼-in (3-cm) square, of smoked salmon
Soy sauce for dipping

❶ Prepare the Basic Sushi Rice.

❷ Prepare the shrimp by blanching them, shelling them, and slicing them in half lengthwise. As an alternative, shell and wash the shrimp and cook them sakamushi style—that is, steamed in sake. Pour just enough sake to cover the bottom of a pan—about 1 tablespoon—plus a little water and a pinch of salt. Add the shrimp and bring the pot to a boil. Reduce the heat to medium and cook, covered, for a few minutes until the shrimp have a nice pink color. Be careful not to scorch or overcook them. You may also microwave the shrimp for 2 minutes with 1 tablespoon of sake in a dish covered with plastic wrap.

❸ Mix the egg, mirin, sugar and salt well in a microwaveable bowl. Microwave the mixture for 1 minute, mix it again with a fork or chopsticks to make it crumbly, and then microwave it for 30 seconds to 1 minute more, until the egg is set. The results should be moist and crumbly.

❹ Divide the Basic Sushi Rice into 16 equal portions of about 1 tablespoon each and lightly shape each portion into a ball.

❺ Cut a 12-inch (30-cm) square of plastic wrap and place one piece of shrimp in the center of it. Spread about ⅛ teaspoon of wasabi on the shrimp, and then place a ball of rice on top of it.

❻ Wrap the plastic wrap tightly around the rice and shrimp and shape the sushi into a ball. Unwrap it and repeat with each of the remaining pieces of shrimp and fish. (Treat ¼ of the egg mixture as the equivalent to one piece of fish.) One piece of plastic wrap may be used to make several balls, but you will need to replace it if it gets sticky or torn. Using a damp muslin cloth instead of plastic is another alternative.

SEARED TATAKI BEEF SUSHI

Japan has developed a taste for beef in recent generations, and its Kobe beef in particular has become world-famous. Even so, most beef eaten in Japan nowadays is imported, especially from Australia. But wherever you buy your beef, here's a delicious way to make it Japanese.

Time 25 minutes plus 1 hour for rice preparation
Makes 15 pieces

10-oz (300 g) beef rump steak, no more than ¾-in (2-cm) thick
Salt and pepper
Bamboo skewers (pre-soaked in water for 30 minutes) (optional)
3 tablespoons sake
3 tablespoons soy sauce
1 clove garlic, thinly sliced
15 nigiri rice balls
2 tablespoons prepared horseradish

1 Lightly sprinkle the beef with the salt and pepper. Thread the meat onto skewers and grill it over an open flame. Because this is a relatively large piece of meat, you will probably need three skewers to hold it. Arrange the skewers in a fan shape and hold them at the point all three of them cross. Cook each side of the beef for about 1 minute or until it is done to your preference. Remove skewers and let the meat rest for 15 minutes. As an alternative to this open-flame method, simply sear the beef on both sides in a very hot skillet. Do this for 30 seconds on each side for rare meat, and longer for medium or well-done.

2 Make a sauce by combining the sake, soy sauce and garlic in a saucepan. Bring it to a boil long enough for the alcohol to evaporate from the sake, and then pour it through a strainer.

3 Slice the beef very thinly.

4 Prepare the nigiri rice balls according to "Nigiri Sushi Basics" (page 32), using the beef in place of fish and about ½ teaspoon of horseradish in place of the wasabi.

5 Serve the Seared Tataki Beef Sushi with the sauce on the side for dipping.

CHICKEN SALAD SUSHI

This is a variation of the gunkan style of sushi, named for its imagined resemblance to a battleship. Usually, a strip of nori is wrapped around a bite-size portion of rice to form a cup that is filled with a loose topping that may be piled up like a battleship's superstructure (see Tuna Tartare Gunkan Sushi on page 109). But in this recipe, the crisp black nori is replaced by cool green cucumber, a more suitable accompaniment to mild chicken salad, especially for those not accustomed to nori.

Time 20 minutes plus 1 hour for rice preparation
Makes 12 pieces

½ **standard quantity Basic Sushi Rice (page 23)**
1 **boneless, skinless chicken breast half**
1 **tablespoon sake**
Dash of salt
1 **teaspoon reserved chicken drippings (from the chicken)**
2 **Japanese cucumbers**
2 **tablespoons minced onion**
2 **tablespoons mayonnaise**
1 **teaspoon lemon juice**
Freshly ground black pepper

❶ Prepare the Basic Sushi Rice.

❷ Lightly sprinkle the chicken with the sake and salt. Microwave for a few minutes until done. Reserve 1 teaspoon of the drippings.

❸ Thinly slice the cucumbers into broad ribbons with a vegetable peeler and soak them in cold water for a few minutes to make them crisp. Pat them dry with paper towel.

❹ Divide the rice into 12 portions and make sushi balls resembling those used for nigiri sushi (see page 32).

❺ Shred the chicken into tiny pieces and mix them with the onion, mayonnaise, lemon juice and reserved chicken drippings.

❻ Wrap a cucumber ribbon around each sushi ball to form a cup, with the cucumber forming the cup's sides and the rice filling most of the interior. Gently flatten the rice at the bottom of the cup with your finger to create a little space for the chicken salad. Fill the cup with a spoonful of chicken salad, sprinkle it with freshly ground pepper, and serve immediately.

TOFU SUSHI POUCHES

Inari, the Japanese deity of rice cultivation, has obvious significance for sushi. But inari sushi, or sushi rice stuffed into a pouch made of fried tofu, is actually named for the foxes that guard Inari's many shrines—usually as pairs of stone statues. According to legend, foxes love fried tofu. Worshippers sometimes leave an offering of inari sushi at the fox statues' paws. Fried tofu, called abura-age, is a specialty product and is typically purchased ready-made. When a piece of it is cut in half, it can be opened out like a pita to create a little bag to be filled with rice.

Time 30 minutes (includes pouch preparation) plus 1 hour for rice preparation
Makes 10 pouches

1 standard quantity Basic Sushi Rice (page 23)
2 tablespoons white sesame seeds, roasted

INARI TOFU POUCHES
(**Makes** 20 pouches)
10 whole pieces fried tofu (abura-age)
1²/₃ cups (400 ml) water
2 tablespoons sake
2 tablespoons mirin
3½ tablespoons sugar
3 tablespoons soy sauce

❶ Prepare the Basic Sushi Rice.

❷ To prepare the Inari Tofu Pouches, rinse the fried tofu pieces to remove the excess oil. Next, boil some water in a pan, cook the fried tofu for about 15 seconds, and then remove and drain.

❸ When the pieces have cooled, cut each piece in half across its middle. Then open up each half like a coin purse, using the cut end as its mouth. If the sides should stick together, roll a round chopstick over them to loosen the insides, and try again. (Any other cylindrical object, such as a bottle or a rolling pin, will work too. To prevent the pouches from tearing, just avoid rolling the fried tofu under anything with an edge, including a chopstick that has a square cross-section.)

❹ Put the water in a pan and add the sake, mirin, sugar and soy sauce. Add the fried tofu pouches. Sink a plate on top of the tofu to keep it from rising to the surface of the liquid. Bring to a boil and then reduce the heat to medium and cook until all the liquid is absorbed, about 10 to 15 minutes. Be watchful so as not to scorch the pouches against the bottom of the pan.

❺ Remove the tofu pouches from the heat and set them aside to cool. Leftover pouches may be refrigerated or frozen.

❻ Gently mix the sesame seeds into the Basic Sushi Rice. Divide the rice into 12 portions and press them lightly into balls.

❼ Fill twelve of the cooked tofu pouches with a rice ball each. Fold the top of each pouch shut in the manner of a paper bag.

CRAB AND AVOCADO SUSHI

In addition to its harmonious mix of colors and flavors, this nigiri also marries the textures of juicy crab, creamy avocado, crisp cucumber and of course chewy sushi rice.

Time 20 minutes plus 1 hour for rice
preparation
Makes 8 pieces

1 Japanese cucumber
1 teaspoon wasabi
8 nigiri rice balls
Sixteen 2-in (5-cm)-long crab
pieces
Eight 2-in (5-cm)-long avocado
slices
Soy sauce for dipping

❶ Using a vegetable peeler, slice 8 long ribbons from the cucumber.

❷ Prepare the nigiri rice balls according to the instructions in "Nigiri Sushi Basics" (page 32).

❸ Top each nigiri rice ball with ⅛ teaspoon of wasabi, a slice of avocado and two pieces of crab.

❹ Use a cucumber ribbon as a "belt" to wrap around each piece of sushi to help hold the ingredients together.

SMOKED DUCK SUSHI WITH ORANGE

A dark slice of smoked duck breast usually has a pale strip of fat running along one edge, which endows this sushi with visual interest plus a succulent texture.

Time 10 minutes plus 1 hour for rice preparation
Makes 8 pieces

8 slices smoked duck breast (about 5 oz/140 g total)
8 nigiri rice balls
2 teaspoons mustard
2 tablespoons minced candied orange peel
1 or 2 chives, cut into thin 1-in (2.5-cm)-long strips
Soy sauce for dipping

❶ Combine one slice of duck with one nigiri rice ball according to the instructions in "Nigiri Sushi Basics" (page 32), substituting ¼ teaspoon of mustard for the wasabi. Repeat for remaining pieces of duck and rice.

❷ Garnish with orange peel and chives.

Spicy Mushroom Sushi, Bamboo Shoot Sushi
and Asparagus Sushi

BAMBOO SHOOT SUSHI

When something is popping up everywhere, Japanese people compare it to "ugo no takenoko," or bamboo shoots after a rain. Real bamboo shoots, called takenoko, can be prepared as a tasty sushi topping in any weather.

24 slices cooked bamboo shoots
    (about 3½ oz/85 g total)
1 teaspoon sake
½ teaspoon mirin
1 teaspoon light soy sauce
1 cup (250 ml) dashi broth
8 nigiri rice balls
1 teaspoon wasabi
8 mitsuba leaves with stems, lightly
    boiled
Soy sauce for dipping

❶ Select commercially available bamboo shoots that come sliced, boiled and packed in water. In a pan, combine the bamboo shoots, sake, mirin, soy sauce and dashi. Cook over medium heat for 5 minutes. Let it stand, uncovered, for another 5 minutes.

❷ Prepare the nigiri rice balls according to the instructions in "Nigiri Sushi Basics" (page 32). Top each one with ⅛ teaspoon wasabi and a slice of bamboo shoot.

❸ Use the mitsuba leaves and stems as "belts" to hold the sushi together. If mitsuba is not available, substitute spring onions or thin green scallions.

Time 15 minutes plus 1 hour for rice preparation   Makes 8 pieces

SPICY MUSHROOM SUSHI

This nigiri combines two elemental flavors, earthy shiitake mushrooms and fiery chili peppers, in one savory vegetarian treat.

6 dried shiitake mushrooms,
    soaked in water overnight
½ cup (125 ml) water reserved from
    soaking mushrooms
1 tablespoon sugar
1 tablespoon mirin
1 tablespoon soy sauce
¼ teaspoon dried red pepper flakes
1 carrot
8 nigiri rice balls
1 teaspoon wasabi
Soy sauce for dipping

❶ Soak the shiitake mushrooms in water for at least 1 hour, but preferably overnight, to soften them. Drain the mushrooms when you are ready to begin cooking, but save ½ cup (125 ml) of the water they have been soaking in. Cut off and discard the knobby root ends of the mushrooms' stems.

❷ In a pan, combine the mushrooms, reserved water, sugar, mirin, soy sauce and dried red pepper flakes. Bring the mixture to a boil and reduce the heat to minimum until the liquid is almost absorbed. Thinly slice the mushrooms.

❸ Using a vegetable peeler, slice eight long ribbons from the carrot. Boil them briefly to soften them. Prepare the nigiri rice balls according to "Nigiri Sushi Basics" (page 32). Top each rice ball with ⅛ teaspoon of the wasabi and a few slices of mushroom. Use the carrot ribbons as "belts" to hold the sushi together.

Time 15 minutes plus 1 hour for rice preparation and several hours to soak mushrooms   Makes 8 pieces

ASPARAGUS SUSHI

These tasty green tidbits are a good example of the modern trend toward diverse sushi that is often seafood-free.

4 thin stalks of asparagus, cut into
    2-in (5-cm)-long pieces
8 nigiri rice balls
1 teaspoon wasabi
8 strips nori seaweed, cut to about
    ⅓ x 6 in (1 x 15 cm)
Soy sauce for dipping

❶ Cook the asparagus in salted boiling water until almost tender.

❷ Prepare the nigiri rice balls according to "Nigiri Sushi Basics" (page 32). Top each rice ball with about ⅛ teaspoon wasabi and 2 pieces of asparagus.

❸ Use a nori strip as a "belt" to wrap around each piece of sushi to help hold the ingredients together.

Time 20 minutes plus 1 hour for rice preparation   Makes 8 pieces

TOFU SUSHI

This scrumptious morsel pushes the sushi envelope with its unconventional, rice-on-top design, yet it is a combination of solidly traditional elements: fried tofu, sushi rice and shiso leaves. These three go remarkably well together, especially if served while the tofu is still warm. The broad, frilly shiso leaves have a distinctly Japanese flavor that falls somewhere between basil and mint. If shiso is not available, you can use fresh basil leaves—the largest you can find—for a different but still delicious and colorful variation.

Time 30 minutes plus 1 hour for rice and tofu preparation
Makes 8 pieces

½ cup (120 g) prepared Basic Sushi
   Rice (page 23)
One 14-oz (400-g) block firm tofu
Oil for deep frying
1 egg
2 to 3 tablespoons cornstarch
8 fresh shiso (perilla) leaves or
   16 basil leaves
Freshly ground black pepper

SWEET SOY DRESSING
1 tablespoon sake
1 tablespoon mirin
1 tablespoon soy sauce
1 teaspoon sugar

❶ Prepare the Basic Sushi Rice.

❷ Press the water from the tofu to make it firmer. To do this, wrap the tofu with a paper towel and place it on a cutting board under a small plate with a weight on top. The weight, roughly 1 pound (500 g), may be a stone no larger than your fist, a coffee mug filled with water, or even a can of soup. Prop up one end of the board so that the water will drain off. (The other end of the board should be in or over a sink.) Let it stand for about 30 minutes and then cut the tofu into 8 bite-size rectangular pieces.

❸ Pour at least 1 inch (2.5 cm) of oil into a saucepan and heat it to 350°F (175°C).

❹ Beat the egg in a small bowl. Dip each tofu piece in the egg, roll it in the cornstarch, and then deep-fry it in the oil until the surface looks golden and crispy. Remove the fried tofu from the oil and let the pieces drain on a paper towel.

❺ Make a deep slit in the center of each piece of fried tofu. Place 1 tablespoon of the Basic Sushi Rice in the center of each shiso leaf and fold the leaf around it. Insert each leaf-wrapped portion of rice into the slit in one piece of tofu.

❻ Prepare the Sweet Soy Dressing by mixing the sake, mirin, soy sauce and sugar in a saucepan and bringing it briefly to a boil. Drizzle the Dressing onto a serving plate and arrange the sushi pieces on top. Sprinkle with freshly ground black pepper.

JAPANESE OMELET SUSHI

Making Japanese omelets is an essential part of the repertoire of a Japanese cook. Block-shaped and slightly sweet, these omelets are sliced up to provide a popular topping for nigiri sushi.

Time 30 minutes plus 1 hour for rice
    preparation
Makes 12 pieces

3 eggs
1 tablespoon mirin
1½ to 2 tablespoons sugar, or to
    taste
Pinch of salt
1 tablespoon vegetable oil
12 nigiri rice balls
Twelve ⅓ x 6-in (1 x 15-cm) nori
    seaweed strips
Soy sauce for dipping

❶ Beat the eggs. Add the mirin, sugar and salt and mix well.

❷ Heat a rectangular Japanese omelet pan until hot. Add a little of the oil and carefully wipe away the excess with a paper towel, leaving the pan barely slick. Add ⅕ of the egg mixture, spreading it evenly over the bottom of the pan. When it is almost set, use a spatula to bunch up the egg at your end of the pan.

❸ Push the cooked egg back to the far side of the pan, oil the pan again and add another ⅕ of the egg mixture, spread evenly over the visible portion of the bottom of the pan. When the egg has set, roll the previously cooked portion of the egg across it toward your side, as if rolling it up in a carpet. Oil the pan and repeat the same process until all of the egg mixture is used up.

❹ Place the cooked omelet on a bamboo mat and roll it up to form an oval shape. When cooled, cut into slices between about ¼ and ½ inch (8 mm) thick.

❺ Prepare the nigiri rice balls according to "Nigiri Sushi Basics" (page 32). Top each rice ball with one slice of omelet. Use the nori strips as "belts" to hold the sushi together.

EGG CAKE SUSHI

In this recipe, an egg-based mixture is baked in a pan, similar to the way one would prepare an Italian frittata. But the inclusion of hanpen fish cake gives the results a distinctly Japanese flavor.

Time 30 minutes plus 1 hour for rice
    preparation
Makes 12 pieces

One 4-oz (100-g) block of hanpen
    (fish cake)
5 eggs
1 tablespoon mirin
2½ tablespoons sugar
⅓ teaspoon salt
12 half-size nigiri rice balls
Soy sauce for dipping

❶ Preheat oven to 350°F (175°C). Line a pan about 7 inches (18 cm) square with parchment paper.

❷ Process the hanpen in a food processor until smooth. Add the eggs, mirin, sugar and salt and continue processing until very smooth. Turn the egg mixture into the pan and bake for about 15 minutes until lightly browned.

❸ When cool, cut the soft egg cake into 12 rectangular pieces. Make a deep slit in the center of each.

❹ Prepare the nigiri rice balls according to the "Nigiri Sushi Basics" on page 32, but make them only half their ordinary size. Nestle a rice ball into the slit in an egg cake piece, continuing until all twelve egg cake pieces are filled.

TEMPURA SUSHI

After sushi, tempura is one of the first things to come to mind when people hear the words "Japanese food." This recipe combines Basic Sushi Rice with deep-fried tempura shrimp and vegetables. When making it, remember that tempura batter should be kept very cold to achieve the lightest and crispiest results.

Time 30 minutes plus 1 hour for rice preparation
Makes 8 servings

½ standard quantity Basic Sushi Rice (page 23)
Vegetable oil for deep-frying
16 very small shrimp, shelled and deveined
½ carrot, peeled and cut into matchstick strips
4 green beans, cut into 1-in (2.5-cm) lengths
1 oz (30 g) lotus root, thinly sliced and soaked in vinegar and water

TEMPURA BATTER

1 egg
1 cup (250 ml) ice-cold water
½ cup (65 g) all-purpose flour

TEMPURA SAUCE

½ cup plus 1½ tablespoons (150 ml) water
3 tablespoons mirin
3 tablespoons soy sauce
½ tablespoon sugar
1 piece dried kelp
⅓ oz (10 g) bonito flakes
1 teaspoon cornstarch dissolved in 2 tablespoons water

❶ Prepare the Basic Sushi Rice. Divide the rice into 16 portions. Mold each portion in a small cup or other container and turn them out onto a plate.

❷ Heat the oil to 350°F (175°C).

❸ To make the Tempura Batter, combine the egg and ice-cold water and mix well. Then add the flour, but mix it only briefly, being sure to leave the batter lumpy.

❹ Dip the shrimp and vegetables one by one in the batter. Deep-fry them in the hot oil until they become golden brown. Drain the hot tempura on a paper towel.

❺ To make the Tempura Sauce, combine the water, mirin, soy sauce, sugar, kelp and bonito flakes in a saucepan and bring to a boil. Pour the sauce through a strainer to remove the kelp and bonito flakes, and then bring it to a boil once again. Add the cornstarch dissolved with water to thicken the sauce. Let simmer briefly.

❻ Put the cooked tempura into the sauce, stir once to give it a light coating, and then arrange the pieces on top of the sushi rice portions.

SMOKED SALMON SUSHI

Lemon juice and capers are classic salmon condiments, and this recipe uses an easy alternative kind of sushi rice that gets its mild acidity from those two ingredients instead of the traditional Sushi Dressing Sauce that is typically used.

Time 20 minutes, plus 45 minutes for preparing rice
Makes 1 loaf or 8 pieces

1 standard quantity Simple White Rice (page 25)
2 tablespoons lemon juice
2 tablespoons capers
1½ tablespoons sugar
3 tablespoons rice vinegar
½ teaspoon salt
6 slices smoked salmon (about 4½ oz/ 125 g total)
Few sprigs of fresh dill for garnish
Few slices of lemon for garnish

❶ Prepare the Simple White Rice. Add the lemon juice and capers, and mix gently but well.

❷ Combine the sugar, rice vinegar and salt in a small bowl and mix well to make a marinade. Soak the smoked salmon slices in the marinade for about 5 minutes.

❸ Use a sheet of plastic wrap to line a narrow container, such as a 3½ x 7 inch (9 x 18 cm) mini pound cake pan that's about 2½ inches (6.25 cm) deep. Use enough plastic wrap so that 4 to 5 inches (10 to 12 cm) extends beyond either side of the container. Arrange the salmon slices so they completely cover the bottom of the container, cutting them to fit if necessary. Cover the salmon with the rice.

❹ Fold the edges of the plastic wrap over the rice and press down firmly to form the sushi into a "cake."

❺ Turn the sushi out onto a serving dish and remove the plastic wrap. Cut it into pieces and garnish with dill and lemon slices.

TERIYAKI CHICKEN SUSHI POUCHES

In Japan, foxes are said to love fried tofu—and the sushi that can be made with it. In the West, foxes are known for sneaking into henhouses for a stolen chicken dinner. This recipe combines it all, using fried tofu Inari sushi as a platform to serve teriyaki chicken.

Time 30 minutes plus 1 hour for rice preparation
Makes 10 pouches

1 standard quantity Basic Sushi Rice (page 23)
10 Inari Tofu Pouches (page 38)
2 tablespoons white sesame seeds
2 boneless chicken thighs, about ¾ lb (350 g) total
1 tablespoon vegetable oil
1 tablespoon sake
1 tablespoon mirin
½ tablespoon sugar
1½ tablespoons soy sauce
3 spring onions or thin green onions (scallions), cut into 2-in (5-cm) pieces

❶ Prepare the Basic Sushi Rice.

❷ Prepare the Inari Tofu Pouches.

❸ Sprinkle the white sesame seeds over the Basic Sushi Rice and mix them in. Divide the rice into 10 equal portions. Mold each portion into a ball and put one in each pouch.

❹ Fold the edges of the pouch halfway down the inside to make a basket-like rim. The rice inside should fill only about half of the pouch, leaving room for the chicken.

❺ To give the chicken skin an attractive brown color, preheat a skillet until it is very hot. Add the oil and put the chicken in skin side down. Cook over high heat until the skin nicely browned. Then, turn the chicken over and pour the sake over it. Cover and cook over low heat for about 5 minutes. When the chicken is almost done, add the mirin, sugar, soy sauce and the white parts of the onions. Continue cooking over medium heat, turning occasionally, until the chicken looks nice and shiny.

❻ Cut each thigh into small pieces. Place the pieces into the basket formed by the top of each tofu pouch. Decorate with the cooked white parts of the onion, and add a little of the green part as well as a further garnish.

CHAPTER TWO

SUSHI ROLLS

Kyushu, the southernmost of Japan's four main islands, is home to some of the world's most enthusiastic rolled sushi lovers. In 2002, at a festival in Saga Prefecture on the island, 2,400 nimble-fingered participants joined forces to create a single sushi roll that was over one mile (1,825 meters) long. The ingredients included over 1,000 pounds (485 kg) of fish and vegetables, a ton of rice, and at least 10,000 sheets of nori, a dried seaweed that resembles crisp black paper. But don't worry—the recipes in this book call for much smaller portions.

If 10,000 sheets sounds like a lot, keep in mind that nori is a major marine crop in Kyushu, and that Japan as a whole produces seven billion sheets of it every year—not to mention the nori harvests of neighboring China and Korea.

Until historically recent times, however, Saga Prefecture's prodigious culinary feat would have been impossible. Japanese people have been eating seaweed for more than 2,000 years, and have been making maki sushi (rolled sushi) for more than 200, but nori was a scarce and expensive ingredient for most of that time. The seaweed, technically a species of red algae, was difficult to cultivate because its method of reproduction was not understood. Harvests were so uncertain that nori was nicknamed "gambler's grass." In fact, the earliest recorded maki sushi recipe didn't use nori as a wrapping at all but instead called for the skin of a fugu blowfish—a fish that is famous for being toxic if incorrectly prepared.

But don't worry about that, either. Most of the sushi rolls in this book are not difficult to make, and none of them are dangerous. In addition to cheap, widely available nori, some of the rolls are wrapped in even easier-to-find lettuce, and a few have no external "skin" at all. Instead, one of them is draped in smoked salmon, another gets a rainbow coating of mixed fish and vegetables, and yet another is encrusted with golden-brown sesame seeds.

To get off to a simple start, try some hoso maki (literally, "thin rolls"), in which sushi rice and one other ingredient, such as cucumber or tuna, are rolled up in a sheet of nori. Once you are comfortable with your basic rolling technique, move up to the slightly more complex decorated rolls, and finally the Flower Roll, which reveals a flower-shaped cross-section when sliced and served.

FOUR COLOR ROLLS

Cheese, avocado, cucumber and crab team up to give this sushi roll its multicolor checkerboard look. For the most visually appealing results, cut and arrange the ingredients with care, and display each slice of the roll with its more attractive side up.

Time 30 minutes plus 1 hour for rice
preparation
Makes 2 rolls

1 standard quantity Basic Sushi
Rice (page 23)
1 avocado, skin and pit removed
½ Japanese cucumber
3½ oz (100 g) cheese
6 imitation crab sticks
2 sheets nori seaweed, about 7 x
8 in (18 x 20 cm)

❶ Prepare the Basic Sushi Rice.

❷ Cut the avocado, cucumber and cheese into strips matching the size and shape of the crab sticks.

❸ Cover a bamboo mat with a sheet of plastic wrap. Place one sheet of nori on it and spread ½ of the rice on the nori, covering it evenly and completely.

❹ Turn the nori over, so that the rice side is resting on the plastic wrap.

❺ Arrange the crab sticks and avocado side by side, close to the near edge of the nori. Arrange the cucumber and cheese on top of the crab sticks and avocado.

❻ Use the mat to carefully roll up the arranged fillings inside the rice and nori. Tug gently on the free end of the mat to tighten it.

❼ Unroll, cover the sushi once again with plastic wrap and cut it into slices. Repeat with the remaining ingredients to make a second roll.

TRADITIONAL NORI TUNA ROLLS

The bright red color of lean tuna (akami) has earned this basic roll its Japanese nickname, tekka-maki, which literally means "flaming iron roll." The bright red fish in the middle of the white rice is said to resemble a glowing bar of iron, hot from a blacksmith's forge. Of course, the tuna itself is not literally hot, because it is fresh and uncooked. If you are working with fresh, uncooked fish for the first time, this is a good, simple recipe to help you get used to it.

Time 10 minutes plus 1 hour for rice
preparation
Makes 4 thin rolls cut into about
two dozen bite-size pieces

2 sheets nori seaweed, about 7 x
8 in (18 x 20 cm)
1 teaspoon wasabi paste
4 oz (100 g) fresh uncooked tuna,
cut into 7-in (18-cm)-long and
½-in (1.25-cm)-thick bars

❶ Prepare the Basic Sushi Rice and divide it into four equal portions.

❷ Cut each nori sheet in half across its longer length. This should give you four pieces of approximately 4 x 7 inches (10 x 18 cm) each.

❸ Place one piece of nori with its shiny side down on a bamboo rolling mat, with one of the nori's longer sides lined up with the near edge of the mat. Spread one portion of Basic Sushi Rice gently and evenly across the nori, leaving about 1 inch (2.5 cm) of nori exposed at the far edge.

❹ Spread ¼ of the wasabi sparingly across the center of the rice. Place a single long bar of tuna across the rice on top of the wasabi. (If no one piece of tuna is long enough, you may place shorter pieces end to end.)

❺ Use the mat to roll up the nori with the rice and tuna inside. Once the sushi is rolled up, firmly grasp the rolled mat and gently tug on its free end to make sure the roll is tight. Unroll the mat and put the rolled sushi on a cutting board.

❻ Slice the roll into pieces 1 to 1½ inches (2.5 to 3.75 cm) thick. Repeat the process with the rest of nori and Basic Sushi Rice to make four rolls.

BARBECUED PORK INSIDE-OUT ROLLS

Juicy sautéed pork and crunchy and yellow peppers are ready to roll—literally and figuratively. Because this sushi roll recipe does not include any nori, there's no worry about it getting soggy if you should pack it in a picnic basket and take it on the road to eat later in the day.

Time 30 minutes plus 1 hour for rice preparation
Makes 2 rolls

1 standard quantity Basic Sushi Rice (page 23)
1½ teaspoons vegetable oil plus more for boiling the peppers
½ yellow bell pepper, cut into strips
½ green bell pepper, cut into strips
Salt and pepper
6 oz (180 g) pork loin, thinly sliced
1 tablespoon sake
1 tablespoon sugar
1 tablespoon vinegar
1 tablespoon soy sauce
2 tablespoons tomato ketchup
1 tablespoon black sesame seeds, roasted
3 or 4 frilly lettuce leaves or other salad greens, torn into very small pieces

❶ Prepare the Basic Sushi Rice.

❷ Boil a pan of water with a few drops of vegetable oil added. Add the yellow and green peppers and boil for 15 seconds, until barely tender. (In this way, the vegetable is cooked to a glossy finish with fewer calories than if it had been sautéed.) Drain.

❸ Warm a skillet and add the 1½ teaspoons of oil. Lightly sprinkle salt and pepper over the pork and stir-fry it until the color of the pork changes. Add the sake, sugar, vinegar, soy sauce and ketchup and cook for 1 minute, stirring constantly. The sauce should thicken slightly.

❹ Mix the sesame seeds into the Basic Sushi Rice. Divide the rice into two portions.

❺ On a board, lay a sheet of plastic wrap over a bamboo mat. Spread one portion of sushi rice on the plastic to form a 6 x 8 inch (14 x 20 cm) rectangle.

❻ Arrange ½ of the lettuce across the center of the rice. Top with ½ of the cooked pork and pepper mixture. Roll the mat tightly to make a roll.

❼ Repeat with the remaining ingredients to make another roll. Cut the two rolls into slices to serve.

TRADITIONAL FUTOMAKI THICK ROLLS

Big, fat sushi rolls, bursting with every imaginable combination of ingredients, are popping up on menus all over the world. Many are newly invented combos using locally popular ingredients, but Japanese futomaki thick rolls, such as this one, are the common ancestors to all of them. In the Kansai region, centered on Osaka, people have a tradition of eating futomaki at Setsubun, an early February holiday that, like Groundhog Day, anticipates the coming of spring.

Time 1 hour and 20 minutes plus
  another hour for rice preparation
Makes 4 big rolls

6 shiitake mushrooms
2 standard quantities Basic Sushi
  Rice (page 23)
1 cup (250 ml) reserved mushroom-
  soaking water
1 tablespoon mirin
1 tablespoon soy sauce
3 tablespoons sugar
3 eggs
Dash of salt
1 tablespoon vegetable oil
3½ oz (85 g) spinach
2 tablespoons Traditional Denbu
  (see recipe below) or canned
  flake tuna or salmon, drained
4 sheets nori seaweed

TRADITIONAL DENBU
(**Makes** 3 tablespoons)
¼ lb (100 g) white fish fillet such
  as cod, sea bream or sole
1 tablespoon sake
1 tablespoon mirin
1 tablespoon sugar
Generous pinch of salt
A few drops red food coloring
  dissolved in a little water
  (optional)

❶ Soak the shiitake mushrooms in 2 cups (500 ml) water for at least 1 hour, but preferably overnight, to soften them. Drain the mushrooms when you are ready to begin cooking, but save 1 cup (250 ml) of the water they have been soaking in. Cut off and discard the knobby root ends of the mushrooms' stems.

❷ Prepare the Basic Sushi Rice.

❸ To prepare the Traditional Denbu, debone and mince the fish. Combine the fish and the rest of the ingredients, including the red food coloring, if using, in a small saucepan. Cook over medium heat, stirring continuously with a strong wire whisk or several chopsticks bundled together for several minutes until fluffy. When it is almost ready, add more salt to taste if desired. Set aside 2 tablespoons of the denbu for this recipe and place the remaining tablespoon in the refrigerator for later use (use within 3 days.)

❹ In a pan, combine the mushrooms, reserved mushroom-soaking water, mirin, soy sauce and 1 tablespoon of the sugar. Bring the mixture to a boil, reduce the heat to its lowest setting, and cook until the liquid is almost absorbed. Thinly slice the mushrooms.

❺ Lightly beat the eggs with the remaining 2 tablespoons of sugar and the salt. Using the beaten egg mixture and the vegetable oil, prepare a Japanese omelet following the recipe on page 47 (Japanese Omelet Sushi). Cut the omelet into ½-inch (1.25-cm)-wide strips.

❻ Boil the spinach in salted water, cut off the root ends of the stems, and drain the spinach very well.

❼ Assemble the roll following the illustrated instructions below. When assembled, remove the mat and, using a very sharp knife and wiping the blade with a damp cloth between each stroke, slice the roll. Repeat the process for the remaining ingredients to make a total of four rolls.

Assembling the Futomaki Roll Place a sheet of nori on a bamboo mat. Spread ¼ of the Basic Sushi Rice on the nori, leaving about 1 inch (2.5 cm) of the edge farthest from you uncovered. Arrange ¼ of the omelet strips, shiitake mushrooms, spinach and denbu or flaked fish across the center of the rice. Roll the ingredients up carefully inside the rice, tightening the mat around the roll.

BROWN RICE SMOKED SALMON ROLLS

The dark, salty flavors of smoked salmon combined with pickled gherkins and nutty brown rice add up to an earthy taste experience that might make you feel as if you were eating on the porch of a log cabin in a cool, piney forest. These Brown Rice Salmon Rolls go nicely with a glass of wine, even a red one.

Time 30 minutes plus 1 hour for rice preparation
Makes 2 rolls

1 standard quantity Brown Sushi Rice (page 25)
10 sprigs fresh dill, chopped
10 baby gherkins
1 sheet nori seaweed, about 7 x 8 in (18 x 20 cm), cut in half
12 slices smoked salmon (about 10 oz/300 g total)
Wasabi

❶ Prepare the Brown Sushi Rice.

❷ Mix the dill into the Brown Sushi Rice. Divide the rice into two large portions.

❸ Place half a sheet of the nori on a bamboo mat. Take ⅓ of one large rice portion and spread it evenly over the nori, leaving about 1 inch (2.5 cm) of nori exposed along the edge farthest away from you—this will be the last edge of the nori to be rolled up.

❹ Line up ½ of the baby gherkins end to end along the center of the rice. Roll up the pickles inside the rice to make a narrow roll. Set this aside.

❺ Place a sheet of plastic wrap over the bamboo mat and spread the remaining Brown Sushi Rice on it in a rectangular shape as wide as the length of the narrow roll. Place the narrow roll on top of this rice and roll it up into a thicker roll with the Brown Sushi Rice on the outside.

❻ On a fresh piece of plastic wrap on the mat, lay out the salmon slices in a row that is the length of the thick roll. The slices should be overlapping, and placed at about a 30-degree angle. Dab them lightly with wasabi.

❼ Unwrap the thick roll and place it on top of the salmon slices. Roll it up in the bamboo mat to give the salmon roll its shape.

❽ Remove the roll from the bamboo mat and plastic wrap, and place it on a cutting board with the salmon side up. Drape it with the plastic wrap again, followed by the bamboo mat. Apply gentle pressure to the bamboo mat along the bottom of the roll, so that the mat pulls the salmon firmly down onto the rice roll and gives the top of the roll a smooth, uniform surface.

❾ Move the mat so that one edge is even with one end of the roll, and tuck in any loose or uneven rice to give the roll a neat appearance. Repeat for the other end of the roll.

❿ Remove the bamboo mat and slice the roll while it is still covered in plastic, using a very sharp knife that you have dampened by wiping with a moist cloth. Then remove the wrap.

⓫ Use the remaining ingredients to repeat the process to make a second roll.

MARINATED TUNA HAND ROLLS

For sheer simplicity, Marinated Tuna Hand Rolls are hard to beat. They are inspired by Korean yukke, a beef tartare dish seasoned with sesame oil and soy sauce. Here, fresh tuna gets the yukke treatment, bathing briefly in a savory marinade and then going straight to the sushi rice.

⅓ standard quantity Basic Sushi Rice (page 23)
4½ oz (125 g) fresh tuna, cut into 8 sticks
4 chives, cut into 4-in (10-cm) lengths
4 sheets of nori seaweed, about 7 x 8 in (18 x 20 cm), cut in half

YUKKE MARINADE
1 tablespoon soy sauce
1 teaspoon sesame oil
½ teaspoon sugar
1 tablespoon white sesame seeds, roasted

❶ Prepare the Basic Sushi Rice.

❷ Mix together all of the ingredients for the Yukke Marinade and marinate the tuna for 5 minutes.

❸ Place 1 to 2 tablespoons of sushi rice just to the right of the center of half a sheet of nori. Arrange one piece of tuna and some chives on the rice.

❹ Lift the lower right-hand corner of the nori, bring it over the ingredients and tuck it under the middle of the left side of the rice. Then roll the remaining loose nori around the fillings like a cone. Repeat with the remaining ingredients to make 8 rolls.

Time 10 minutes plus 1 hour for rice preparation time   **Makes** 8 rolls

SEASONED SHRIMP ROLLS

Visually, this roll is the opposite of the Rainbow Roll. While that one is extravagantly colorful, this one is understatedly pale. But they both call for similar techniques, and they both display their star ingredients on top—and both of them are delicious.

Time 30 minutes plus 1 hour for rice preparation
Makes 2 rolls

1 standard quantity Basic Sushi Rice (page 23)
8 to 10 fresh medium-size shrimp, heads removed
4 tablespoons sake
Dash of salt
2 tablespoons wasabi paste (vary to taste)
Soy sauce for dipping

❶ Prepare the Basic Sushi Rice.

❷ Insert a toothpick lengthwise through each shrimp to prevent it from curling up while cooking. Place the shrimp in a saucepan with the sake and salt. Cover and cook over medium heat for 1 to 2 minutes until done.

❸ When the shrimp are cool enough to comfortably handle, remove the toothpicks and shell the shrimp. Make a deep incision along the shrimp's undersides so that you can open them up and flatten them out like a hinge or a book.

❹ Cover a bamboo mat with plastic. Put ½ of the sushi rice on the plastic and shape it into an 8-inch (20-cm)-long bar in the center of the mat. Roll the mat up and tighten it to make the bar's thickness even. Unroll it and set the rice bar on a cutting board.

❺ Dab a bit of wasabi along the top of the rice bar. Arrange about ½ of the flattened shrimp neatly on the rice bar, placing them at a 45-degree angle to the bar. Cover with plastic wrap and a bamboo mat and use these to shape and slightly flatten the bar. Try not to press straight down on the sushi. Instead, as with the Rainbow Roll, exert pressure along the bottom edges of the mat so that it pulls the shrimp downward onto the rice and gives the top of the roll a smooth surface.

❻ Remove the mat. Cut into bite size pieces through the plastic wrap. Remove the wrap and serve.

❼ Repeat with the remaining rice and shrimp to make a second roll.

ROAST BEEF AND ASPARAGUS ROLLS

The use of asparagus as a sushi ingredient is said to be a British invention. But a far more iconically British food is a mouthwatering slab of juicy roast beef with a dab of stimulating horseradish on the side. In this Anglo-Japanese recipe, roast beef and asparagus come together in sushi, with horseradish standing in for wasabi.

Time 30 minutes plus 1 hour for rice preparation
Makes 2 rolls

1 standard quantity Basic Sushi Rice (page 23)
4 tablespoons finely chopped watercress stems
3 stalks asparagus, boiled in salted water
5 oz (150 g) thinly sliced roast beef
2 teaspoons horseradish
5 or 6 watercress leaves for garnish

FRAGRANT CITRUS SAUCE
2 tablespoons yuzu juice or lemon juice
½ teaspoon grated yuzu peel or lemon peel
2 teaspoons soy sauce
1 teaspoon sugar

❶ Prepare the Basic Sushi Rice.

❷ Mix the finely chopped watercress stems with the Basic Sushi Rice. Divide the rice into two portions.

❸ Place a sheet of plastic wrap over a bamboo mat. Spread one of the portions of rice to cover a rectangular area about 7 inches (18 cm) square. Place ½ of the asparagus in the center of the rice and roll up the rice around it. Tighten the mat around the roll by holding the rolled-up mat with one hand and gently pulling at the mat's free end with the other. The resulting roll should look like a solid white cylinder of rice.

❹ Remove the plastic wrap from the roll and dab a little horseradish all along the top of the roll. Then, layer ½ of the roast beef diagonally along the length of the roll. Work your way down the roll, placing each piece at the same 45-degree angle to the roll, allowing the pieces to overlap enough to cover the rice.

❺ Drape the roll with the plastic wrap again, followed by the bamboo mat. For this step, don't actually roll it again. Instead, leave it upright (beef on top) and apply gentle pressure to the bamboo mat along the bottom of the roll, so that the mat pulls the toppings firmly down onto the rice roll and gives the top of the roll a smooth, uniform surface.

❻ Repeat with the remaining ingredients to make a second roll.

❼ Mix all of the ingredients for the Fragrant Citrus Sauce, and serve it alongside the rolls. Garnish the top of the rolls with the watercress leaves.

BROWN RICE CALIFORNIA ROLLS

Farmers rather than fishermen are to thank for colors and textures—crunchy orange carrot, creamy green avocado, and chewy flavorful cheese—that make up this good-tasting and good for you vegetarian feast. And as if the fillings weren't healthy enough, the nutty Brown Sushi Rice adds an extra wallop of vitamins. It's a must-try item for those who shy away from fish, but even seafood lovers will find these sushi rolls hard to resist.

Time 30 minutes plus 1 hour for rice preparation
Makes 2 rolls

1 standard quantity Brown Sushi Rice (page 25)
½ carrot, peeled
½ Japanese cucumber
1½ oz (40 g) Monterey Jack or other natural cheese
½ avocado
1 teaspoon wasabi
2 tablespoons mayonnaise
2 or 3 leaves of frilly green lettuce, torn into very small pieces
5 tablespoons (50 g) white or golden sesame seeds, roasted

❶ Prepare the Brown Sushi Rice.

❷ Cut the carrot, cucumber, cheese and avocado into ½-in (1.25-cm)-thick sticks.

❸ Cover a bamboo mat with plastic wrap and spread ½ of the rice onto it, covering a rectangular area of about 5 x 8 inches (13 x 20 cm). Be sure to spread the rice evenly, and keep the edges of the rectangle as neat as possible.

❹ Mix the wasabi with the mayonnaise and spread it in a line across the center of the rice. Place the lettuce, carrots, cucumber, cheese and avocado on top of each other along the line.

❺ Roll up the vegetables inside the rice, and tighten the bamboo mat to firm up the roll. (Be careful not to get any of the plastic wrap caught inside the roll.)

❻ Put the sesame seeds in a dish or shallow container. Take the roll out of the mat and roll it gently back and forth in the seeds until it is thoroughly coated.

❼ Repeat with the remaining rice. Slice up the two rolls and arrange them on a serving plate.

RAINBOW ROLLS

True to their name, Rainbow Rolls come in many colors. In addition to the main ingredients listed here—tuna, bream and avocado—many other variations are possible. A long strip of bright red tuna may be substituted for the green cucumber on the inside, and you can try other toppings such as red and white crab sticks or pinkish-orange salmon. To give the bream a less fishy taste, you may prefer to marinate it for several minutes in lemon juice and olive oil in a small bowl, sprinkled with a bit of salt and pepper. Other fish may be marinated, too, but doing so will sacrifice some of their vibrant color and fresh taste. Bream, however, is white to begin with so marinating does not significantly change its appearance.

Time 50 minutes plus 1 hour for rice preparation
Makes 2 large rolls

1 standard quantity Basic Sushi Rice (page 23)
1 sheet nori seaweed, about 7 x 8 in (18 x 20 cm), cut in half
1 Japanese cucumber, sliced lengthwise into quarters (only 2 quarters will be used)
2 teaspoons wasabi paste (vary to taste)
8 thin slices fresh sashimi-quality tuna (4½ oz/125 g total)
8 thin slices fresh sashimi-quality sea bream or red snapper (4½ oz/125 g total)
½ ripe avocado, cut into 8 slices
Soy sauce for dipping

❶ Prepare the Basic Sushi Rice. Divide the rice into two portions.

❷ Place half a sheet of the nori on a bamboo mat. Take ⅓ of the rice portions and spread it evenly over the nori, leaving about 1 inch (2.5 cm) of nori exposed along the edge farthest away from you—this will be the last edge of the nori to be rolled up. Place a strip of cucumber in the center of the rice, spread some wasabi paste alongside it, and roll the nori and rice around the cucumber to create a narrow roll. Set the roll aside.

❸ Place a piece of plastic wrap on the bamboo mat and spread the remaining ⅔ of the first portion of rice over an area about 6 inches (15 cm) deep and the same width as the length of the small roll you have just made. While spreading the rice with the fingers of one hand, make a "wall" with the other hand to hold the plastic down and keep the edges of the rice neat.

❹ Place the cucumber roll that you have already made in the center of the rice and roll up the rice around it, using the mat and plastic wrap, to make a bigger roll. Tighten the mat around the roll by holding the rolled-up mat with one hand and gently pulling at the mat's free end with the other. The resulting roll should look like a solid white cylinder of rice. If any black nori is showing through, simply patch those spots with a little extra rice and roll again.

❺ Remove the plastic wrap from the roll and dab a little wasabi all along the top of the roll. Then, layer about ½ of the thinly sliced tuna, sea bream and avocado diagonally along the length of the roll. Work your way down the roll, placing each piece at the same 45-degree angle to the roll, allowing the pieces to overlap enough to cover the rice. Try to keep the angle consistent, and alternate the ingredients as you go.

❻ Drape the roll with the plastic wrap again, and then drape the bamboo mat over top. For this step, don't actually roll it again. Instead, leave it upright (main ingredients on top) and apply gentle pressure to the bamboo mat along the bottom of the roll, so that the mat pulls the toppings firmly down onto the rice roll and gives the top of the roll a smooth, uniform surface.

❼ Move the mat so that one edge is even with one end of the roll, and tuck in any loose or uneven rice to give the roll a neat appearance. Repeat for the other end of the roll.

❽ Remove the bamboo mat and slice the roll while it is still covered in plastic, using a very sharp knife that you have dampened by wiping with a moist cloth. Then remove the wrap. Each piece will have at least two colors on top because of the slanting arrangement of the sliced ingredients, and the cross-section will also show the green cucumber and black nori inside.

❾ Use the remaining ingredients to repeat the process to make a second roll. The two leftover strips of cucumber can be cut up for a salad.

TWO-CHEESE TUNA SALAD ROLLS

A tuna salad sandwich with a slice of cheese is a classic American comfort food. But there's no reason why even this humble ingredient combination can't be made over as a sophisticated sushi dish—and look great doing it, too.

Time 30 minutes plus 1 hour for rice preparation
Makes 2 rolls

1 standard quantity Simple White Rice (page 25)
1 tablespoon lemon juice
1 small can flake tuna in oil (about 3 oz/80 g)
2 tablespoons finely minced onion
2 tablespoons mayonnaise
Dash of black pepper
5 or 6 sprigs fresh parsley
4 sandwich slices American cheese
4 sandwich slices cheddar-style cheese

❶ Prepare the Simple White Rice.

❷ Add the lemon juice to the cooked rice. Mix gently but thoroughly.

❸ Prepare the tuna salad by draining the excess oil from the canned tuna. Mix the tuna with the onion, mayonnaise and pepper.

❹ Place a sheet of plastic wrap on a bamboo mat on a board. Divide the rice into two portions and spread one of them evenly on the plastic wrap, forming a rectangle of about 5½ x 8 inches (14 x 20 cm).

❺ Arrange ½ of the tuna salad across the center of the rice. Place ½ of the parsley on top of the salad. Roll the sushi and tighten with the mat.

❻ Take the roll out of the mat and place it on a cutting board. Cut each of the cheese slices in half, for a total of 16 pieces. Arrange 8 of the pieces on top of the rolled rice, positioning them at a slight angle to the roll. The pieces should slightly overlap, with colors alternating.

❼ Cover the sushi with plastic wrap and a mat. Gently press to form the rounded shape of the roll. Remove the mat and cut the roll into slices through the plastic wrap. Remove the wrap before serving. Repeat with the remaining ingredients to make a second roll.

VEGETARIAN THIN ROLLS

To make proper Japanese cucumber rolls, you must use proper Japanese cucumbers, which are nearly seedless and only about 1-inch (2.5-cm) thick. This simple and refreshing roll is known in Japanese as a kappa-maki, named after the magical green creatures called kappa who are said to inhabit Japan's lakes and rivers. Amphibious humanoids with webbed fingers and beaked faces, kappa may be depicted as either menacing or cute, but in either case cucumbers are said to be among their favorite foods. In this recipe, sliced avocado is a good substitute.

Time 10 minutes plus 1 hour for rice preparation
Makes 4 thin rolls cut into about two dozen bite-size pieces

1 standard quantity Basic Sushi Rice (page 23)
2 Japanese cucumbers
1 tablespoon salt
2 sheets nori seaweed, about 7 x 8 in (18 x 20 cm)
1 teaspoon wasabi paste

❶ Prepare the Basic Sushi Rice.

❷ Rinse the cucumbers, rub them with the salt, and roll them back and forth a few times under your palm on a wooden cutting board before rinsing them off again. This process, called "itazuri," adds a little flavor and brings out the cucumber's green color. Slice the cucumbers in half lengthwise, for a total of four long pieces.

❸ Cut each nori sheet in half across its longer length. This should give you four pieces of approximately 4 x 7 inches (10 x 18 cm) each.

❹ Divide the Basic Sushi Rice into 4 equal portions. Place one piece of nori with its shiny side down on a bamboo rolling mat, with one of the nori's longer sides lined up with the near edge of the mat. Spread one portion of Basic Sushi Rice gently and evenly across the nori, leaving about 1 inch (2.5 cm) of nori exposed at the far edge.

❺ Spread ¼ of the wasabi sparingly across the center of the rice. Place a piece of cucumber across the rice on top of the wasabi.

❻ Use the mat to roll up the nori with the rice and cucumber inside. Once the sushi is rolled up, firmly grasp the rolled mat and gently tug on its free end to make sure the roll is tight. Unroll the mat and put the rolled sushi on a cutting board.

❼ Slice the roll into pieces 1 to 1½ inches (2.5 to 4 cm) thick. Repeat the process with the rest of the nori and Basic Sushi Rice to make a total of four rolls.

CAPRESE HAND ROLLS

Basil, tomatoes and mozzarella are a classic combination from the island of Capri—hence the name "Caprese" for salads and other dishes that combine them. In this recipe, shiso leaves from the islands of Japan play basil's roll in a startlingly delicious Shiso Pesto. Any leftover Shiso Pesto may be frozen for future use on salads or pasta. If you don't have any shiso on hand, revert back to fresh basil leaves—but double the number of leaves, as basil leaves are smaller than shiso leaves.

⅓ standard quantity Basic Sushi Rice
    (page 23)
4 sheets nori seaweed, about 7 x 8 in
    (18 x 20 cm), cut in half
8 shiso leaves
8 ohorry tomatoes, cut in half
4 oz (100 g) mozzarella cheese,
    sliced into 8 pieces

SHISO PESTO
20 shiso leaves
3 tablespoons grated Parmesan cheese
1 clove garlic
2 tablespoons pine nuts, roasted
3 tablespoons extra virgin olive oil
Salt to taste (omit if using very
    salty cheese)

❶ Prepare the Basic Sushi Rice.

❷ Process all of the Shiso Pesto ingredients in a food processor until smooth.

❸ Place 1 to 2 tablespoons of sushi rice just to the right of the center of half a sheet of nori. Arrange a shiso leaf, two tomato halves, a piece of cheese, and a spoonful of Shiso Pesto on the rice.

❹ Lift the lower right-hand corner of the nori, bring it over the ingredients and tuck it under the middle of the left side of the rice. Then roll the remaining loose nori around the fillings like a cone. Repeat with the remaining ingredients to make 8 rolls.

Time 15 minutes plus 1 hour for rice preparation time
Makes 8 rolls

CHAPTER THREE

SUSHI SALADS

Compared to bite-size nigiri sushi, hearty chirashi sushi is relatively unknown in the West. That's a shame, because chirashi sushi, which means "scattered sushi," is served up by the generous bowlful with nearly any combination of ingredients that may appeal to you, and it is by far the easiest kind of sushi to make. It might be described as a rice salad, and it is a sushi style that is wide open to imaginative improvisation.

Despite chirashi's casual nature, it has a respectable sushi pedigree, dating back at least as far as the 1700s. Moreover, it is one of many basic Japanese dishes claimed as local specialties on both sides of the Kanto-Kansai culinary divide. People in the Kanto region (centered on Tokyo) and those in the Kansai region (centered on Osaka) often have slightly different ways of preparing simple dishes, with each side believing its way is best.

The basic distinction in the case of chirashi sushi is that the Tokyo style usually has its ingredients arranged on top of a bowl of sushi rice, while the Osaka one usually calls for mixing the ingredients into the rice. But this is far from a hard-and-fast rule, and you will find chirashi sushi prepared either way in both cities. Some of the recipes in this section take advantage of both techniques, mixing in some ingredients while reserving others to decorate the surface.

Though preparing a bowl of chirashi sushi is simple, there are still a few considerations to keep in mind.

For one thing, don't go overboard when mixing the rice. Turn and fold it gently so that most of the individual grains of rice retain their integrity and don't get mashed into a pulp.

Another thing to remember is that presentation is important in Japanese cuisine. Try to pick out a serving bowl or platter whose color or pattern complements the look of your ingredients—especially if you intend to serve your chirashi sushi as a one-dish meal.

Chirashi sushi is fit to enjoy all year round, but it is interesting to know that it is also a highlight of the traditional menu for the Hina Matsuri, or Doll Festival, held each spring on March 3. On this day, families with daughters display collections of elegant dolls—often precious heirlooms—and pray for their daughters to grow up strong and healthy. Perhaps a nutritious bowl of chirashi sushi will help that wish come true.

TOKYO STYLE SUSHI RICE SALAD

Shogun Ieyasu Tokugawa made history in 1603 when he moved the seat of Japan's government from the magnificent city of Kyoto to a distant fishing town in eastern Japan called Edo. His new capital thrived, and in 1868 it changed its name from Edo to Tokyo (which means "Eastern Capital"). City residents whose roots stretch back for generations are proud to call themselves Edokko (literally, "Children of Edo") rather than Tokyoites, and the buying, selling and eating of fish is still a vital part of the city's economic and cultural life. Tokyo-style sushi, reflected in this recipe, tends to highlight bright red pieces of fresh-from-the-waterfront tuna.

Time 45 minutes plus 1 hour for rice preparation.
Serves 4 to 6 people

2 standard quantities Basic Sushi Rice (page 23)
4½ oz (125 g) fresh tuna, cut into ½-in (1.25-cm) cubes
1½ teaspoons soy sauce
About 1 tablespoon sake
2 pinches of salt
5 oz (150 g) fresh or frozen shrimp, shelled and rinsed
3 eggs
1 tablespoon mirin
1½ to 2 tablespoons sugar, or to taste
4 or 5 sprigs of mitsuba, cut into 1-in (2.5-cm) lengths

1 Prepare the Basic Sushi Rice.

2 Marinate the tuna in the soy sauce for 5 minutes.

3 Prepare the shrimp by cooking them sakamushi style—that is, steamed in sake. Pour just enough sake to cover the bottom of a pan—about a tablespoon—plus a little water and a pinch of salt. Add the shrimp and bring the pot to a boil. Reduce the heat to its lowest setting and cook, covered, for a few minutes until the shrimp have a nice pink color. You may also microwave the shrimp for 2 minutes with 1 tablespoon of sake in a dish covered with plastic wrap. After the shrimp are cooked, cut them into ½-inch (1-cm) pieces.

4 Use the eggs, mirin, sugar and 1 pinch of salt to prepare a Japanese omelet following the instructions provided in the recipe for Japanese Omelet Sushi (page 47). When finished, cut the omelet into ½-inch (1-cm) cubes.

5 Mix the tuna, shrimp and omelet cubes into the Basic Sushi Rice. Turn into a serving dish and sprinkle with the mitsuba stems.

TUNA AND AVOCADO SUSHI RICE SALAD

Hawaiians, like the Japanese, have a long history of enjoying ultra-fresh fish straight from the ocean. One of the islands' most popular traditional dishes is poke, a sashimi-like fish salad that inspired this chirashi sushi or "bowl" sushi recipe.

Time 30 minutes plus 1 hour for rice preparation
Serves 2 to 3 people

1 standard quantity Brown Sushi Rice (page 25)
4 oz (100 g) fresh, sashimi-quality tuna
1 tablespoon soy sauce
½ tablespoon sesame oil
½ avocado, cut into small cubes
1 bunch kaiware daikon or broccoli sprouts

❶ Prepare the Brown Sushi Rice.

❷ Cut the tuna into small, bite-size slices and marinate for at least 10 minutes in the soy sauce and sesame oil.

❸ Gently mix the tuna and avocado into the Brown Sushi Rice.

❹ Turn into a plate and sprinkle with the sprouts.

SIMPLE MUSHROOM AND CHICKEN SUSHI RICE

A gift of globalization, the eringi mushroom was virtually unknown in Japan before the 1990s, but now it is a common sight in supermarkets. It is sometimes grilled in butter at izakaya (Japanese pubs) and is also a popular stir-fry ingredient. Originally native to the Mediterranean, this thick, pale, chewy mushroom can also be found in the English-speaking world under such names as king oyster mushroom, royal trumpet mushroom, or eringi mushroom.

Time 30 minutes plus 1 hour for rice
    preparation
Serves 2 people

1 standard quantity Basic Sushi
    Rice (page 23)
1 boneless, skinless chicken breast
    half
4 medium-size eringi mushrooms
    (about 5-in/12.5-cm long)
Dash of salt
Dash of pepper
Drizzle of olive oil
3 tablespoons minced fresh water-
    cress leaves and tender part of
    stems
4 sprigs of watercress to garnish

ZINGY MARINADE

2 tablespoons white wine vinegar
1 teaspoon sugar
½ teaspoon salt
1 teaspoon Dijon mustard with
    seeds

1 Prepare the Basic Sushi Rice.

2 Cut any tendons from the chicken and pound the breast to a uniform thickness so that heat will penetrate them evenly while they are cooking. Cut the mushrooms to 2-inch (5-cm) lengths and then slice those to about ⅛-inch (3-mm) thick.

3 Arrange the chicken and mushrooms on a metal baking tray and lightly sprinkle them with the salt, pepper and olive oil. Broil for several minutes until the chicken is done (when the juice run clear).

4 As soon as the chicken is cool enough to comfortably handle, shred the meat into small bits. Tear the mushrooms into narrow strips.

5 Prepare the Zingy Marinade by mixing the white wine vinegar, sugar, salt and mustard. Add the chicken and mushrooms, stir them until they are thoroughly coated, and leave them to marinate for about 5 minutes.

6 Gently mix the minced watercress into the Basic Sushi Rice.

7 Pour the marinated chicken and mushrooms over the rice and mix them in gently.

8 Turn the rice into a serving dish and garnish with fresh green sprigs of watercress.

"SCATTERED TOPPING" SUSHI RICE SALAD

This recipe is a classic example of chirashi sushi. The sushi rice is combined with other ingredients that are "scattered" throughout it or across it rather than sitting neatly on top or being rolled up cozily inside. Chirashi sushi is a good family-style sushi because it can be prepared in quantity and presented in a large serving bowl in the middle of the table. It is also very much a freestyle category, with cooks at liberty to add almost any ingredient that takes their fancy. The recipe on this page is an example of gomoku, or "five-kind," chirashi, a category named for the idea that it contains a little bit of everything.

Time 50 minutes plus 1 hour for rice preparation and several hours to soak shiitake mushrooms
Serves 4 to 6 people

- 2 standard quantities Basic Sushi Rice (page 23)
- 4 dried shiitake mushrooms, soaked in 2 cups (500 ml) water until tender
- 1 small carrot
- 4½ oz (125 g) lotus root (about 4-in (10-cm)-long piece of root depending on thickness)
- 1 tablespoon vinegar
- ¾ cup (150 ml) reserved mushroom-soaking water
- 1 tablespoon sake
- 1½ tablespoons soy sauce
- 2 tablespoons plus 1 teaspoon mirin
- 1½ tablespoons plus 1 teaspoon sugar
- 1 egg
- Dash of salt
- 1 oz (30 g) snow peas, stems removed
- 3½ oz (85 g) crab meat (about 7 imitation crab sticks), cut into 1-in (2.5-cm)-long pieces

❶ Prepare the Basic Sushi Rice.

❷ Soak the dried shiitake mushrooms in water for at least 1 hour, but preferably overnight, until they are tender. Drain them, and reserve ¾ cup (150 ml) of the water in which they have been soaking. Trim off the knobby ends of the stems and finely slice the mushrooms.

❸ Peel the carrot and cut it into matchsticks. Peel the lotus root and cut it into small pieces. Soak the lotus root in some water with the vinegar added for five minutes before cooking to avoid discoloration.

❹ Pour the mushroom-soaking water into a saucepan and add the shiitake mushrooms, carrot and lotus. Also add the sake, soy sauce, 2 tablespoons of the mirin and 1½ tablespoons of the sugar. Bring the mixture to a boil, lower the heat to low and cook until most of the liquid has been absorbed.

❺ Mix the egg with the remaining 1 teaspoon of mirin, the remaining 1 teaspoon of sugar, and the salt in a microwave-safe bowl. Microwave for 1 minute and mix well with a fork. Microwave once again for another 30 seconds and mix once again, this time thoroughly to make a very finely crumbled egg.

❻ Boil the snow peas briefly in salted water, then drain them and cut them into very thin slices.

❼ Add the mushrooms and other cooked vegetables with their liquid to the Basic Sushi Rice. Mix gently but thoroughly. Turn the rice into a serving dish and top it with the snow peas, scrambled eggs and crab meat.

BEEF AND CELERY SUSHI RICE SALAD

Beef and celery go well in a sauté. The results go well in a bowl of Brown Sushi Rice for a hearty dish of chirashi sushi mixed sushi. An alternative to celery is the long, woody root of the burdock, called gobo in Japanese, but this tough vegetable has to be cooked for a few minutes longer to become tender.

1 standard quantity Brown Sushi Rice (page 25)
4½ oz (125 g) beef loin, thinly sliced
1 stalk celery (or ½ burdock root)
1 tablespoon peeled and minced fresh ginger
2 tablespoons mirin
2 tablespoons soy sauce
1½ tablespoons sugar
2 spring onions or thin green onions (scallions), chopped

❶ Prepare the Brown Sushi Rice.

❷ Cut the beef slices into small pieces. Cut the celery into thin slices. In a pan, combine the ginger, mirin, soy sauce and sugar. Add the celery and cook for 1 minute. Add the beef and cook until all the liquid is absorbed.

❸ Mix the beef and vegetables into the rice. Turn it into a serving dish and sprinkle it with the chopped spring onions.

Time 30 minutes plus 1 hour for rice preparation
Serves 2 to 3 people

TUNA SUSHI RICE SALAD

"A view of greenery. A wild cuckoo. The first bonito." With these three images, haiku poet Sodo Yamaguchi (1642–1716) evokes the feeling of late spring. Bonito, called "katsuo" in Japanese, are smaller cousins of the tuna. They are migratory fish that move northward up the coast of Japan in the spring and early summer and head south again in the autumn. The first bonito catch of the year was a happy event in Yamaguchi's day, and gourmets in modern Japan eagerly welcome it, too. Ginger, rather than wasabi, is the traditional bonito accompaniment, and this chirashi sushi mixed sushi recipe includes a sub-recipe you can use to make your own ginger pickles to mix right in. (You may also buy the pickles ready-made.)

2 standard quantities Basic Sushi Rice (page 23)
2 oz (50 g) drained Pickled Ginger (page 25)
1 bonito tuna fillet or other tuna fillet (about 8 to 10 oz/300 g)
2 tablespoons soy sauce
2 tablespoons mirin
2 tablespoons gold or white sesame seeds, roasted
8 spring onions or thin green onions (scallions), finely chopped

❶ Prepare the Basic Sushi Rice.

❷ Cut the ginger pickles into thin matchsticks. Add them to the rice and mix gently.

❸ Cut the bonito fillets into small pieces, about ¼-inch (6 mm) thick. Marinate the fish in the soy sauce and mirin for about 10 minutes.

❹ Add the bonito and its marinade to the rice. Sprinkle it with the sesame seeds and most of the spring onions and mix thoroughly but gently.

❺ Serve the mixed sushi in bowls, sprinkling on the remaining spring onions as garnish.

Time 30 minutes plus 1 hour for rice preparation and ginger marinating time
Serves 4 to 6 people

TRADITIONAL TOPPINGS ON SUSHI RICE

Sushi is not always about raw fish, but the freshest fruits of the sea certainly have their place in sushi cuisine. This seafood topping sushi recipe puts an assortment of fresh ingredients—tuna, shrimp, scallops and roe—proudly on display. This dish embodies the most famous characteristics of Japanese cuisine in that it uses the freshest available ingredients and presents them in a beautiful visual arrangement.

1 standard quantity Basic Sushi Rice (page 23)
4 oz (100 g) fresh tuna, cut into sashimi slices
½ tablespoon soy sauce
6 to 8 fresh whole ama-ebi shrimp or 3 medium-size shrimp
3 fresh scallops
1 oz (30 g) tobiko (flying fish roe) or salmon roe
A few kaiware daikon sprouts or broccoli sprouts, cut into small pieces

WASABI DRESSING SAUCE

3 tablespoons rice vinegar
½ teaspoon sugar
1½ tablespoons soy sauce
1 tablespoon vegetable oil
1 teaspoon freshly grated wasabi or wasabi paste

❶ Prepare the Brown Sushi Rice.

❷ Slice the tuna, preferably sashimi-style (see pages 28–29), and dip one side of each slice in the soy sauce in a small bowl or saucer to give the fish the lightest possible coat of the sauce. Carefully wash, shell and drain the ama-ebi sweet shrimp. If you're using medium-size shrimp, shell and devein them and then boil them until just done. Then cut each medium-size shrimp in half lengthwise. Cut each scallop in half—into two discs of even thickness, not two semicircles.

❸ Place the Basic Sushi Rice on a serving platter. Arrange the seafood and tobiko attractively on top of it and sprinkle it with the sprouts.

❹ Prepare the Wasabi Dressing Sauce by mixing the rice vinegar, sugar, soy sauce, vegetable oil and wasabi. Serve the sushi with the sauce on the side.

Time 30 minutes plus 1 hour for rice preparation
Serves 2 to 3 people

CEVICHE SUSHI RICE BOWL

Making ceviche is an art and science. This Peruvian dish combines vegetables and fresh fish with a citrus marinade that chemically "cooks" the fish without any heat. The citric acidity of ceviche is analogous to the vinegary acidity of sushi rice, and the two elements make a natural combination in this sushi recipe.

1 standard quantity Simple White Rice (page 25)
3½ oz (85 g) white fish fillets, such as sea bream or sole
1 tablespoon rice vinegar
½ tablespoon sugar
2 tablespoons finely minced onion
1 tablespoon lemon juice
1 tablespoon olive oil
4 tablespoons roasted and coarsely chopped macadamia nuts (from about 17 nuts)
4 cherry tomatoes, minced
3 or 4 sprigs of Italian parsley, chopped

❶ Prepare the Simple White Rice.

❷ Slice the fish fillets into small, thin pieces.

❸ Mix together the vinegar, sugar, onion, lemon juice and olive oil. Marinate the fish in this lemon juice mixture for at least 10 minutes or up to half a day. (Note, however, that the texture of the fish will become tougher the longer it marinates.)

❹ Gently mix the marinated fish, macadamia nuts, tomatoes, and parsley into the rice.

Time 20 minutes plus 45 minutes for rice preparation
Serves 2 to 3 people

GRAPEFRUIT AND PINEAPPLE SUSHI RICE SALAD

This sweet, colorful and vitamin-rich chirashi sushi ("scattered" or mixed sushi) is one for which it is not necessary to prepare the Basic Sushi Rice because the lemon-based dressing and the fruits' own natural acidity do the job of turning ordinary rice into sushi rice for you. Light and relatively effortless, this sushi makes a good weekend breakfast to be washed down with a cup of hot or iced tea.

Time 15 minutes plus 45 minutes for rice preparation
Serves 4 to 5 people as a light meal

1 standard quantity Simple White Rice (page 25)
½ fresh grapefruit
⅛ fresh pineapple
1 tablespoon lemon juice
2 teaspoons sugar
4 to 8 mint leaves for garnish

❶ Prepare the Simple White Rice.

❷ Peel the grapefruit and separate it into wedges, and cut them into very small pieces. Cut the pineapple into small pieces. The total amount of fresh cut fruit should be about 1 cup (200 g).

❸ Mix the lemon juice and sugar in a bowl. Add the fruits, along with their juice.

❹ Pour the fruit and juice mixture over the warm rice and mix gently.

❺ Garnish with the mint leaves.

PROSCIUTTO AND ROASTED PEPPER SUSHI RICE

A fresh, crunchy, slightly sweet yellow bell pepper seems like the very picture of natural perfection. But it can be improved upon. Roasting a bell pepper takes a little work, but it pays big dividends in the form of glistening, succulent, slightly sweet flesh. This chirashi sushi mixed sushi recipe calls for the roasted pepper to be marinated with sun-dried tomatoes, with the marinade itself finally providing the vinegary acidity to "sushify" the rice.

Time 30 minutes plus 45 minutes for rice preparation
Serves 4 people

- 1 standard quantity Simple White Rice (page 25)
- 1 large yellow bell pepper
- 1 tablespoon white wine vinegar
- 1 teaspoon sugar
- 2 tablespoons minced sun-dried tomatoes (packed in olive oil)
- 4 slices prosciutto ham, cut into bite-size pieces
- 3 or 4 sprigs of Italian parsley for garnish

❶ Prepare the Simple White Rice.

❷ Roast the yellow bell pepper. The simplest way to do this is to hold the pepper in an open flame with a pair of tongs until the skin is charred. Alternatively, you may blacken the pepper on a grill or under a broiler, placing it as close to the heat source as possible so that the skin chars without burning the tender flesh inside. Be sure to turn the pepper so that all sides are completely blackened.

❸ Immediately after charring the pepper, put it in a plastic bag or a covered bowl—in other words, a container that will hold in moisture and heat with minimal ventilation while sitting on a tabletop or counter. Allow the pepper to sweat in its mini-sauna for about five minutes to loosen its skin.

❹ Take the pepper out of the container, peel off the skin and remove the stems and seeds. Remove any stubborn bits of skin with a knife. Chop the succulent flesh into small pieces.

❺ Mix the vinegar and the sugar. Add the minced tomatoes and the chopped roasted pepper. Let the vegetables marinate for about 5 minutes.

❻ Pour the marinated vegetables and their sauce over the warm rice. Mix gently.

❼ Turn the rice onto a serving platter and garnish with the prosciutto and the parsley.

POACHED EGG SUSHI RICE SALAD

Japan may have more than its fair share of earthquakes and volcanoes, but the upside of living in such a geologically active country is an abundance of natural hot springs called "onsen." A visit to a hot spring resort is a popular way for people to unwind on the weekend. A popular snack on such a trip, often enjoyed in a scenic setting such as a mountain gorge or rocky shore, is an onsen tamago, or "hot spring egg," that is poached inside its shell through long immersion in the scalding water. If you don't happen to have a hot spring nearby, you can still make ordinary poached eggs and enjoy them on top of this sushi with bacon and olives.

Time 30 minutes plus 45 minutes for rice preparation
Serves 3 people

1 standard quantity Simple White Rice (page 25)
2 or 3 slices bacon
1 tablespoon lemon juice
12 pitted black olives, minced
1 cup (80 g) finely sliced or shredded lettuce or endive
3 eggs

BALSAMIC SAUCE
2 tablespoons balsamic vinegar
½ teaspoon soy sauce
1 teaspoon sugar (optional)

❶ Prepare the Simple White Rice.

❷ Microwave the bacon slices on a paper towel for 1 to 2 minutes until crisp. Break into small pieces.

❸ Add the lemon juice to the cooked rice and mix gently. Then, gently mix in the olives and bacon.

❹ Prepare the Balsamic Sauce by mixing the balsamic vinegar and soy sauce in a small saucepan. The sweetness of balsamic vinegar varies, so taste a drop and add about a teaspoon of sugar if you would like it sweeter. Simmer the sauce over low heat for 1 or 2 minutes (or microwave it) until it is slightly thickened.

❺ Line three plates with the shredded lettuce or endive and then top each one with ⅓ of the lemon-flavored rice. Make a little indentation in the top of each serving of rice to make room for a poached egg.

❻ Make three poached eggs. To do this, crack each egg into its own microwaveable cup. Prick the yolks a few times with a fork, and gently pour 1 tablespoon of very hot water over each egg. Microwave for up to a minute until cooked but still soft. Drain off the water.

❼ Set each poached egg into the top of a portion of rice. Drizzle with the Balsamic Sauce and serve.

CHAPTER FOUR

SUSHI PARTY

Attractive presentation is a key element of Japanese cuisine. At the high end, a meal at an elegant restaurant can be a leisurely exercise in art appreciation, as one petite dish after another is served on its own carefully chosen plate, arranged and garnished just so. On a more modest level, schoolchildren opening bento boxed lunches packed by their mothers may find strips of vegetables and nori seaweed arranged on a shallow bed of rice to form the face of a favorite cartoon character. In either case, food should please the eye before it pleases the tongue.

The recipes in this section are all designed to please the eye, from the tidy shapes of oshi sushi (pressed sushi) such as Layered Vegetable Sushi to the fanciful garnish of Grilled Eel Sushi, which visually alludes to Japanese folklore.

Of course, Japanese food is not limited to sushi, and these recipes reach out to borrow from other branches of the nation's cuisine, such as tempura (shrimp and vegetables deep-fried in a light batter), sukiyaki (thinly sliced beef simmered in a savory sauce), and tsukemono (pickled vegetables that come in almost infinite variety).

Several of these recipes use a molded block of Basic Sushi Rice as a pedestal on which to display the other ingredients. Feel free to use a mold in your favorite shape, and arrange the sushi in a way that pleases you. Other recipes tuck the rice away inside of a package, such as the inari sushi and egg-wrapped sushi recipes.

Inari, a traditional way of serving sushi rice inside a pouch made of fried tofu, is popular among kids because the pouches are soft, chewy and just a little sweet. As a simple snack, it can be made with nothing but Basic Sushi Rice and the pouches themselves, but the recipes in this book jazz things up a bit with additions ranging from sesame seeds to teriyaki chicken.

Compared to inari sushi, egg-wrapped sushi is a relatively modern technique, yet it looks very traditional because the bright yellow sheet of egg that contains the rice and other ingredients like a sack visually suggests a furoshiki, the colorful wrapping cloth that most Japanese once used to carry their everyday items. (Think of it as the Vuitton bag of bygone generations.)

The newest material to be added to the sushi-wrapping category is thinly sliced cucumbers, used here to make an elegant package for smoked salmon. And here's an important tip: If you serve this eye-pleasing sushi to any guest who declares it is too pretty to eat, simply urge them on by promising to make more.

CUCUMBER PARCELS WITH SMOKED SALMON

Sushi is usually not eaten with a knife and fork. But an exception can be made for these generous portions, which come wrapped up like birthday presents in cucumber ribbons, with capers in place of bows. Cut into one and you'll find a layer of smoked salmon running through dill flavored rice—what a tasty surprise.

Time 30 minutes plus 45 minutes for rice preparation
Makes 6 large pieces

1 standard quantity Basic Sushi Rice (page 23)
6 to 8 sprigs fresh dill
2 Japanese cucumbers
Salt
4 slices smoked salmon (about 3 oz/80 g total), cut into bite-size pieces
18 small capers for garnish

❶ Prepare the Basic Sushi Rice. Finely chop the dill and mix it gently into the rice.

❷ Rinse the cucumbers, rub them generously with salt and roll them back and forth under your hand on a cutting board so that the salt penetrates them, which helps to heighten their green color. Rinse them again, and then slice them lengthwise into ribbons with a vegetable peeler and set them aside. Each cucumber should make about a dozen ribbons, for a total of 24.

❸ Lay 2 slices of cucumber closely side by side, with another 2 slices perpendicular to them. The 4 slices should overlap in a woven pattern. For best results, work on the plates on which you plan to serve the sushi.

❹ Divide the rice into 6 equal portions. Fill a Japanese teacup or similar rounded container that is about 3 inches (7.5 cm) wide with ½ of one portion of the Sushi Rice. Press the rice lightly into place and lay a few pieces of salmon on it before covering it with the other ½ of the rice portion. (To keep rice from sticking, rinse the cup first or line it with plastic wrap.)

❺ Turn the rice and salmon cake out onto the center of the woven cucumber. Fold the ends of the cucumber ribbons over the top of the rice to cover it completely.

❻ Repeat the process for each of the remaining portions of rice, and garnish with capers.

SUSHI RICE EGGROLLS WITH CREAM CHEESE

Grilled eel is a traditional summer food in Japan, and thus an ideal filling for picnic-ready egg-wrapped sushi. Grilled eel fillets sold commercially often come with a coating of dark, sweet Kabayaki Sauce, and bottled sauce is also available.

Time 40 minutes plus 1 hour for rice preparation
Makes 10 pieces

1 standard quantity Basic Sushi Rice (page 23)
4 oz (100 g) grilled eel with Kabayaki Sauce
2 oz (50 g) cream cheese, cut into ¼-in (6-mm) dice
10 Egg Sheets (see Egg-Wrapped Sushi with Mushrooms, page 113)
10 tiny sprigs of sansho leaves for garnish (optional)

❶ Prepare the Basic Sushi Rice.

❷ Japanese eels almost always come precooked. In this case, cut it into small pieces and allow it to marinate in its own sauce. If the eel is not precooked, grill it over an open flame for a few minutes on each side, brushing it lightly with Kabayaki Sauce (using the recipe from Grilled Eel Sushi, page 120). When it is done, cut it into small pieces.

❸ Mix the eel and the cream cheese with the Basic Sushi Rice. Divide the rice mixture into 10 portions and gently form them into oval-shaped rice balls.

❹ Make the Egg Sheets.

❺ Place a rice ball in the middle of an Egg Sheet, flatten it slightly, and wrap it neatly. Repeat with the remaining rice balls and Egg Sheets. Optionally, garnish with tiny sprigs of sansho leaves or other fresh herbs.

PROSCIUTTO ROLLS

As its Italian name suggests, prosciutto is not a traditional Japanese food. But you might find that hard to believe if you were to drop in at a Tokyo restaurant or grocery store these days. Known as nama hamu (literally, "fresh ham"), it is now turning up everywhere in Japan—on pizzas, in sandwiches and tossed into salads. Here it gets a starring role in sushi, standing in for the nori that usually wraps things up.

½ standard quantity Simple White Rice (page 25)
½ tablespoon lemon juice
8 slices prosciutto ham, approximately 4 x 3 inches (10 x 7 cm)
2 oz (50 g) blue cheese, crumbled
½ apple, cut into sticks
4 or 5 lettuce leaves, torn into small pieces, for garnish

WALNUT SAUCE
1 tablespoon white wine vinegar
1 teaspoon sugar
½ teaspoon soy sauce
½ teaspoon olive oil
1 tablespoon roasted and finely chopped walnuts

❶ Prepare the Simple White Rice. Mix in the lemon juice while the rice is freshly cooked and still warm. Divide the rice into 8 portions.

❷ Lay a piece of prosciutto flat on a bamboo mat. If its length and width are noticeably different, place it so that it appears vertical to you.

❸ Spread one portion of rice on the ham, leaving about 1 inch (2.5 cm) uncovered on the edge farthest from you. Arrange ⅛ of the blue cheese and apple sticks across the center of the rice. Roll the ham and rice up carefully and tighten the roll with the mat.

❹ Repeat with the remaining ingredients to make eight rolls. Cut each roll in half and arrange them on a plate with some lettuce as a garnish.

❺ Prepare the Walnut Sauce by combining the white wine vinegar, sugar, soy sauce and olive oil. Mix thoroughly, and then add the walnuts. Serve the Walnut Sauce alongside the prosciutto rolls for dipping.

Time 20 minutes plus 45 minutes for rice preparation   **Makes** 16 pieces

TUNA SALAD ROLLS

Reinventing the classic tuna sandwich with rice and seaweed instead of bread, this common thin roll is made with easy-to-find ingredients (and no raw fish). The mayonnaise in the tuna salad may not look like a traditional Japanese condiment, but it is a fully naturalized one, having been produced industrially in Japan since at least 1925. Nowadays, a squeeze bottle of the stuff is one of the standard supplies for a Japanese home or restaurant kitchen.

Time 10 minutes plus 1 hour for rice preparation
Makes 4 thin rolls cut into about two dozen bite-size pieces

1 standard quantity Basic Sushi Rice (page 23)
1 small can tuna in oil, about 3 oz (80 g)
2 sheets nori seaweed, about 7 x 8 in (18 x 20 cm), cut in half across its longer lengths to yield 4 pieces
2 tablespoons minced onion
2 tablespoons mayonnaise
Dash of freshly ground black pepper

❶ Prepare the Basic Sushi Rice.

❷ Drain excess oil from the tuna. To prepare the tuna salad, mix the tuna with the minced onion, mayonnaise and pepper. Divide into 4 portions.

❸ Divide the Basic Sushi Rice into 4 equal portions. Place one piece of nori with its shiny side down on a bamboo rolling mat, with one of the nori's longer sides lined up with the near edge of the mat. Spread one portion of the rice gently and evenly across the nori, leaving about 1 inch (2.5 cm) of nori exposed at the far edge. Spread one portion of the tuna salad on the rice.

❹ Use the mat to roll up the nori with the rice and tuna salad inside. Once the sushi is rolled up, firmly grasp the rolled mat and gently tug on its free end to make sure the roll is tight. Unroll the mat and put the rolled sushi on a cutting board

❺ Slice the roll into pieces between 1 to 1½-inches (2.5 to 4-cm) thick. Repeat the process with the rest of the nori and Basic Sushi Rice to make a total of four rolls.

SUSHI CANAPÉS

Most Japanese use chopsticks to eat their sushi, but it is well within the bounds of good etiquette to use your fingers. In fact, some Japanese gourmets actually prefer to eat it that way. These sushi canapés make an inviting finger food for everyone, as they are served in miniature pastry cups that guests can pick up without getting any rice stuck to their fingers. And the six assorted flavors—from mango to bacon—include choices that appeal that gourmets from any country.

Time 1 hour for rice preparation plus 10 minutes for each canapé recipe (plus 30 minutes to marinate salmon roe for Salmon Roe Canapé)
Makes 24 canapé-size cups in total

1 standard quantity Simple White Rice (page 25)
1½ to 2 tablespoons lime or lemon juice
24 ready-to-use unsweetened mini pie shells or shallow pastry cups (about 2-in/5-cm) wide

❶ Prepare the Simple White Rice.

❷ Add the lemon or lime juice to the warm, freshly cooked rice and mix gently but thoroughly. The acidity of citrus juice can vary depending on conditions in the place the fruit was grown. For best results, add just 1½ tablespoons of the juice, mix well and have a little taste. Add more juice, up to 2 tablespoons in total, according to your preference.

❸ Fill the pastry cups with 1 tablespoon of the rice.

❹ Add toppings of one or more of the six canapé combinations that follow. Each canapé recipe makes four canapés.

PROSCIUTTO AND MELON CANAPÉ

4 bite-size or smaller pieces melon
2 slices fresh prosciutto ham, cut in half
4 rice-filled canapé cups (see recipe above)
Small piece chervil or parsley for garnish

Wrap each piece of melon in half a slice of prosciutto. Place each piece on a rice-filled cup and garnish with chervil or parsley.

SALMON ROE CANAPÉ

2 oz (50 g) fresh salmon roe
½ teaspoon soy sauce
½ teaspoon mirin
4 rice-filled canapé cups (see recipe above)
4 fresh shiso leaves

Marinate the salmon roe in the soy sauce and mirin for at least 30 minutes in your refrigerator. Place each shiso leaf on a portion of rice and top with a spoonful of the marinated salmon roe.

Crab Stick Salad Canapé

Smoked Salmon Canapé

Mango and Mint Canapé

BLT Canapé

CRAB STICK SALAD CANAPÉ

**2 imitation crab sticks or 1 oz (30 g) fresh cooked
crab meat**
1 tablespoon mayonnaise
⅛ teaspoon soy sauce
**7 or 8 kaiware daikon sprouts or broccoli sprouts,
chopped**
4 rice-filled canapé cups (see page 107)

Shred the crab sticks or crab meat into small pieces.
Make a crab salad by combining the mayonnaise and
soy sauce with the crab meat and mixing well. Mix in
the sprouts, and place ¼ of the salad on each of the 4
rice-filled cups.

MANGO AND MINT CANAPÉ

½ mango, thinly sliced
4 rice-filled canapé cups (see page 107)
4 sprigs of fresh mint

Arrange the mango slices on the four rice-filled cups
and garnish with the fresh mint.

SMOKED SALMON CANAPÉ

4 strips smoked salmon, about 1 x 4 in (3 x 10 cm)
4 rice-filled canapé cups (see page 107)
4 tiny sprigs of fresh dill
4 small pieces of lemon peel

Roll up each strip of salmon to form a rose. Place one
salmon rose on each canapé and garnish with the dill
and lemon peel.

BLT CANAPÉ

1 slice bacon, chopped
1 frilly green lettuce leaf
2 cherry tomatoes
4 basil leaves
4 rice-filled canapé cups (see page 107)

Fry the chopped bacon in a skillet until crisp, or place
it on a paper towel on a plate and microwave it for 1
minute. Drain any excess fat. Tear the lettuce into at
least four pieces and cut the tomatoes in half. Arrange
¼ of the bacon and lettuce pieces, 1 basil leaf and half
a tomato on each of the 4 rice-filled cups.

TUNA TARTARE GUNKAN SUSHI

"Gunkan" means battleship in Japanese. A strip of nori running around a nigiri rice ball like a wall forms the imaginary vessel's hull, while the sushi toppings—in this case a dollop of fresh tuna-walnut salad—are said to resemble a ship's superstructure.

Time 20 minutes plus 1 hour for rice preparation
Makes 8 pieces

4½ oz (125 g) fresh tuna
2 teaspoons soy sauce
2 tablespoons roasted and finely chopped walnuts
2 spring onions or thin green onions (scallions), chopped
8 nigiri rice balls
8 strips nori seaweed, cut to about 1¼ x 6 in (3 x 15 cm)
Soy sauce for dipping

❶ Chop or mince the tuna and mix in the soy sauce. Add the walnuts and onions.

❷ Make the nigiri rice balls according to "Nigiri Sushi Basics" (page 32).

❸ Wrap one strip of nori around each rice ball to form a small cup, with the nori as the sides of the cup and the rice as its floor. To keep the ends of the nori strips from flapping loose, you may secure them with a dab of "glue" made by crushing a grain or two of Basic Sushi Rice between your fingers.

❹ Use a spoon to fill each cup with the tuna, onion and walnut mixture.

YAKITORI SUSHI SKEWERS

Outside of suburban commuter train stations in Japan you will often find a yakitori joint. It's a restaurant or bar specializing in grilled chicken on a stick, often sold through a sidewalk window to tired workers on their way home. Because it is so portable, yakitori is popular at Japanese festivals and picnics, too. One favorite variety combines chicken with chunks of naganegi long Japanese leeks. This recipe takes that idea and adds chewy balls of sushi rice.

Time 30 minutes plus 1 hour for rice preparation
Makes 10 sticks

½ standard quantity Basic Sushi Rice (page 23)
10 wooden skewers, at least 6-in (15-cm) long
7 oz (200 g) chicken thigh, cut into at least 10 bite-size pieces
½ Japanese leek (naganegi), cut into 1½-in (4-cm) pieces
Dash of ground red pepper (cayenne) for garnish

YAKITORI SAUCE
6 tablespoons mirin
6 tablespoons soy sauce
4 tablespoons sugar

❶ Prepare the Basic Sushi Rice.

❷ Soak the wooden skewers in water. (This keeps them from burning on the grill later.)

❸ Microwave the chicken pieces for 2 minutes until nearly done.

❹ Shape the Basic Sushi Rice into 20 round, slightly flattened balls. (One way to do this is to place a bite-size portion of Basic Sushi Rice in a piece of plastic wrap and twist the wrap tightly around it to make a ball, then press on it with your thumb to slightly flatten it.)

❺ Arrange the rice balls, Japanese leek and nearly cooked chicken pieces on the skewers. Continue until all are skewered. (Put the skewers through the flattened sides of the rice balls.)

❻ Make the Yakitori Sauce by combining the mirin, soy sauce and sugar in a pan and cooking over medium heat until slightly thickened

❼ Grill the yakitori on a barbecue or other hot grill, turning occasionally, until the chicken is fully cooked. Brush the skewered ingredients several times with the Yakitori Sauce while cooking.

EGG-WRAPPED SUSHI WITH MUSHROOMS

A good way to make sushi "portable" is to equip it with a durable skin that will last long enough for you to take it on a picnic or to a party. Inari tofu pouches are one common technique. A more fun and colorful solution is to wrap your sushi in a bright yellow sheet of cooked egg.

Time 45 minutes plus 1 hour for rice preparation
Makes 10 parcels

1 standard quantity Basic Sushi Rice (page 23)
4 shiitake mushrooms, soaked in 1 cup (250 ml) water and finely chopped
¾ cup (150 ml) reserved mushroom-soaking water
1 tablespoon sake
2 tablespoons mirin
1½ tablespoons sugar
1½ tablespoons soy sauce
10 tablespoons vegetable oil
10 mitsuba stems or long chives, blanched for 5 seconds in boiling water

EGG SHEETS

3 eggs
½ tablespoon sugar
Dash of salt
½ teaspoon katakuriko or cornstarch
½ tablespoon sake

❶ Prepare the Basic Sushi Rice.

❷ Soak the shiitake mushrooms in water for at least 1 hour, but preferably overnight. Drain the mushrooms, but reserve ¾ cup (150 ml) of the water in which they have been soaking. Remove and discard the knobby root ends of the mushrooms' stems and mince the mushrooms.

❸ Combine the shiitake mushrooms in a pan with the mushroom-soaking water, sake, mirin, sugar and soy sauce. Bring to a boil, lower the heat and cook the shiitake until almost all the liquid is absorbed.

❹ Mix the shiitake mushrooms gently but thoroughly into the Basic Sushi Rice.

❺ To prepare the Egg Sheets, lightly beat the eggs, add the sugar and salt and mix well. Dissolve the katakuriko or cornstarch in the sake, add it to the egg mixture, and lightly beat again.

❻ Heat a 6-inch (15-cm) skillet and add 1 tablespoon of the vegetable oil. Wipe off excess oil and pour enough of the egg mixture to thinly cover the entire bottom of the pan, as if making a crepe. When the egg sheet appears dry, flip it over and briefly heat the other side. Turn it out onto a zaru strainer or other mesh surface so air can circulate around it as it cools. Repeat the process until you have 10 egg sheets.

❼ Divide the sushi rice into 10 portions and lightly form them into rice balls.

❽ Place one rice ball into the center of an egg sheet, gather the edges of the sheet together to form a bag, and tie the bag shut with a mitsuba stem or chive. Repeat the process with the remaining ingredients to make 10 egg sushi parcels.

COCKTAIL SUSHI

One fun thing about going out for cocktails with friends is that everybody can enjoy something different. One person might relish a Tom Collins while another savors eggnog and a third sips from a Cosmopolitan. All it takes is a good mixologist behind the bar to make everyone happy. This recipe allows you to put your own mixing skills to work by stirring (not shaking) a variety of ingredients into sushi rice and serving the results in cocktail glasses—a unique presentation to surprise and delight your guests.

1 standard quantity Basic Sushi Rice (page 23)

TUNA COLLINS
1½ oz (40 g) fresh tuna, cut into small dice
1 teaspoon soy sauce
½ avocado, cut into small pieces
A few broccoli sprouts or kaiware daikon sprouts, cut into small lengths, for garnish

EGG NOG
1 egg
1 tablespoon sugar
Dash of salt
1 teaspoon mirin
4 sprigs of chervil or parsley for garnish

CHEESE-MOPOLITAN
⅓ Japanese cucumber, finely diced (1 oz/30 g)
1 oz (30 g) tomatoes, finely diced
1 oz (30 g) Monterey Jack or other natural cheese, finely diced

❶ Prepare the Basic Sushi Rice. Divide it into 3 portions.

❷ To make the Tuna Collins sushi, marinate the diced tuna in the soy sauce for 5 minutes. Add the tuna and the avocado to one portion of the Basic Sushi Rice. Mix gently and divide the rice among four cocktail glasses (or other serving dishes). Garnish with the sprouts.

❸ To make the Egg Nog sushi, mix the egg, sugar, salt and mirin in a microwave-safe bowl. Microwave for 1 minute and mix well with a fork. Microwave once again for another 30 seconds and mix once again, this time thoroughly with a fork to make a very fine scrambled egg. Gently mix the egg into the second portion of Basic Sushi Rice and divide it among four cocktail glasses (or other serving dishes). Garnish each with a sprig of chervil or parsley.

❹ To make the Cheese-mopolitan sushi, gently mix the diced cucumber, tomatoes and cheese into the third portion of Basic Sushi Rice. Divide the rice among four cocktail glasses (or other serving dishes).

Time 30 minutes plus 1 hour for rice preparation
Makes 12 glasses

MARINATED FISH SUSHI

Whole fresh soybeans, or edamame, are a popular summer snack in Japan. Boiled, salted and served up by the bowlful while still in their pods, these beans are fun to eat—just squeeze the pod and out they pop! In this recipe, the soybeans are used to add color, crunch and extra flavor to the sushi rice, creating a green-and-white polka-dot platform for a serving of marinated aji, a common Japanese salt-water fish usually described as "horse mackerel" in English. The firm flesh of an aji, unlike that of a true mackerel, is relatively light in color, making tai sea bream or red snapper good substitutions if aji is not available.

Time 80 minutes plus 1 hour for rice preparation
Makes 4 servings

½ standard quantity Basic Sushi Rice (page 23)
2 horse mackerel, sea bream or red snapper fillets, deboned
1 tablespoon plus 1 teaspoon salt
1 cup (120 g) fresh or frozen soy beans pods or ½ cup (85 g) shelled soy beans
½ cup (125 ml) vinegar
2 shiso leaves sliced into threads for garnish (see "Making Shiso Threads" below)

HORSE MACKEREL MARINADE
2 tablespoon rice vinegar
1 tablespoon sugar

❶ Prepare the Basic Sushi Rice.

❷ Sprinkle the fish fillets with salt on both sides, using about 1 tablespoon in total. Leave them in a flat container for 30 minutes. (If the air in your kitchen is above 65°F (20°C), leave the salted fish in the refrigerator.

❸ If using fresh soybeans, remove the pods from any branches, wash them off and put them in a pan. Sprinkle the pods with 1 teaspoon of the salt and let them stand for a few minutes. Pour hot water over them and boil them on the stove until the beans are tender, about 5 minutes. In the case of frozen beans or peas, simply thaw them out and remove the pods.

❹ Mix the beans into the rice.

❺ Put the vinegar into a bowl and use it to wash the salt off the fillets. Do not discard the vinegar.

❻ Prepare the Horse Mackerel Marinade by mixing the vinegar and sugar in a flat-bottomed container. Marinate the fish fillets for at least 30 minutes (or as long as a day in the refrigerator). When you are ready to make the sushi, peel the skin off the fillets, starting from the head end. Cut the fish diagonally into slices. (See "Slice Your Fish Cleanly" on pages 28–29.)

❼ Wet a round, open-ended kitchen mold about 4 inches (10 cm) in diameter and place it in the center of a serving plate. Fill it with ¼ of the rice and bean mixture and press lightly to create a flat surface. Remove the mold and arrange ¼ of the sliced fish on top of the rice. Decorate with ¼ of the thinly sliced shiso threads, and repeat the process with the remaining ingredients on three more plates.

MAKING SHISO THREADS

MAKING SHISO THREADS: Wash the shiso leaves in water, and then wrap them in a paper towel and squeeze them gently to absorb excess moisture. Finely slice the shiso leaves by cutting them in half lengthwise, rolling them up, and then folding them in half again to give yourself some volume to work with. Then, using a sharp knife, slice the thimblelike mass of leaves as finely as possible to create threadlike strips. *Note:* In Japan, shiso is a standard accompaniment for sashimi, so a sprinkling of delicate green shiso threads may be used as an optional garnish on any sushi that includes raw fish as an ingredient.

MIXED VEGETABLE TOFU SUSHI POUCHES

The abura-age tofu pouches used in inari sushi recipes are naturally sweet, but this recipe adds some savory flavor notes and textural complexity with carrots, lotus root and shiitake mushrooms.

Time 40 minutes (including pouch preparation) plus 1 hour for rice preparation
Makes 10 pouches

1 standard quantity Basic Sushi Rice (page 23)
10 Inari Tofu Pouches
3 dried shiitake mushrooms, soaked in 1 cup (250 ml) water
⅓ cup (80 ml) reserved mushroom-soaking water
½ carrot
2 oz (60 g) lotus root
1 tablespoon sake
1½ tablespoons mirin
1 tablespoon sugar
1 tablespoon soy sauce

❶ Prepare the Basic Sushi Rice.

❷ Prepare the Inari Tofu Pouches by following steps 2 through 5 on page 38.

❸ Soak the dried shiitake mushrooms for at least 1 hour, but preferably overnight, to soften them. When you are ready to begin cooking, drain the mushrooms but set aside ⅓ cup of the water they have been soaking in. Cut off the knobby root ends of the stems and mince the mushrooms.

❹ Peel and mince the carrot and lotus root.

❺ In a pan, combine the reserved mushroom-soaking water with the sake, mirin, sugar and soy sauce. Add the mushrooms, carrot and lotus root, bring the pan to a boil and then reduce the heat to simmer until nearly all liquid is absorbed—about 15 minutes. Pour the cooked vegetables over the Basic Sushi Rice and mix well.

❻ Divide the rice into 10 portions and put each portion into a tofu pouch. Fold each pouch closed. Cut a few of them in half to reveal a cross-section for an attractive presentation.

GRILLED EEL SUSHI

The Milky Way, flowing across the night sky like a river of stars, is called Ama no Gawa (River of Heaven) in Japanese. According to legend, this river separates two lovers, embodied by the stars Altair and Vega, who are allowed to meet only once a year, during the summer festival of Tanabata. Meanwhile, down here on Earth, many Japanese people eat river-dwelling eel at the height of summer in the belief that its nutrients will help them endure the sweltering heat. This recipe combines the two traditions. Eel is the star ingredient, while the optional garnish is inspired by a rippling river design that Japanese schoolchildren are taught to cut from paper as a Tanabata decoration.

Time 40 minutes (longer if starting with uncooked eel) plus 1 hour for rice preparation
Makes 4 servings

½ standard quantity Basic Sushi Rice (page 23)
1 grilled eel (unagi kabayaki) with sauce
1 oz (30 g) green beans, cooked and cut into 2-in (5-cm)-long strips, for garnish
4 fresh sansho leaves (or other tiny-leafed herb) for garnish

RIVER RIBBON GARNISH (OPTIONAL)
1 fresh spring roll wrapper (about 8 in/20 cm square)
Oil for deep-frying

HOMEMADE KABAYAKI SAUCE
2 tablespoons sake
3 tablespoons mirin
1½ tablespoons sugar
3 tablespoons soy sauce

❶ Prepare the Basic Sushi Rice.

❷ Divide the rice into four portions, and shape each portion into a disk-like platform using a moistened 4-inch (10-cm) open-ended circular kitchen mold.

❸ To make the optional River Ribbon Garnish, cut the spring roll wrapper into four long strips. Fold each strip in half along its longer axis and then fold it in half again the same way for a long, narrow shape. With scissors or a knife, make a series of cuts at about ½-inch (1.25-cm) intervals along one side of each strip. Repeat the process on the other side of each strip so that the cuts on either side alternate. Heat the oil to 350°F (175°C). Unfold each strip and briefly deep-fry until lightly browned, using chopsticks to gently stretch them out into a lattice shape as they cook. Drain them on a paper towel.

❹ Bottled Kabayaki Sauce is available, but to make your own simply combine the sake, mirin, sugar and soy sauce in a pan and simmer over low heat for 5 minutes or until slightly thickened.

❺ If the eel is not precooked, brush it lightly with the Kabayaki Sauce and grill it over an open flame for a minute or two on each side. Cut the eel into four long strips, and cut these into 1-inch (2.5-cm) squares. Place on a plate and microwave for 1 or 2 minutes, until they are warm. Arrange the warm eel pieces on top of the rice.

❻ Decorate with the green beans, Kabayaki Sauce, River Ribbon Garnish, if using, and the sansho leaves or other fresh herbs.

COLORFUL SWEET PICKLE SUSHI

Tsukemono, or pickles, are a major category of Japanese cuisine. Every region of the nation has its own special pickling techniques, using a range of substances such as vinegar, salt, miso, soy sauce or even sake lees to preserve virtually every vegetable grown or known. For this sushi recipe, you'll make an easy batch of mixed pickles in advance, and then combine them with rice that has been "sushified" with sweet raspberry vinegar. The crisp, tangy results can be served as dainty appetizers that nicely complement a glass of dry champagne.

Time 35 minutes plus 45 minutes for rice preparation and 6 hours to marinate pickles
Makes 20 bite-size pieces

1 standard quantity Simple White Rice (page 25)
2 tablespoons raspberry vinegar
1 tablespoon sugar
Heaping ½ teaspoon salt
3 tablespoons (30 g) walnuts, roasted and crushed or finely chopped
About 3½ oz (85 g) Sweet Japanese Pickles

SWEET JAPANESE PICKLES
(**Makes** 14 oz/400 g pickles)
1 thin Japanese cucumber, cut into small pieces
¼ large carrot, cut into thin slices or into a flower shape
4 oz (100 g) white or purple cauliflower, separated into small flowerets
2 oz (50 g) lotus root, peeled and cut into thin slices (optional)
1 cup (250 ml) water
⅓ cup (80 ml) rice vinegar
6 tablespoons sugar
½ tablespoon salt

❶ Prepare the vegetables for the Sweet Japanese Pickles. Keep in mind that the smaller you make them, a greater variety of them will fit on top of one piece of sushi. The lotus root should be boiled for 1 minute, or until crisp but tender, and drained. The other vegetables may be boiled if you wish.

❷ To prepare the pickling marinade, combine the water, vinegar, sugar and salt in a saucepan. Bring the mixture to a boil. Remove the pan from the heat and add the prepared vegetables. Marinate the vegetables for at least 6 hours.

❸ Prepare the Simple White Rice.

❹ Mix the raspberry vinegar, sugar and salt to make a dressing. Stir until the sugar is fully dissolved. Pour the dressing over the hot cooked rice and mix it in gently but thoroughly. Then mix in the walnuts.

❺ Use plastic wrap to line a tray of mini cupcake molds. Divide the rice into 20 portions and shape each portion in the molds, pressing the rice gently so it sticks together without being crushed. Any other round mold, no more than 2 inches (5 cm) across will also do. (If there's nothing else available, you might even improvise with an ice cube tray.) Turn the rice portions out of the mold and arrange them on a serving platter.

❻ Top each piece of sushi with a few pieces of drained Sweet Japanese Pickles (about 3½ oz/85 g in total.)

> ## PICKLE TIP
>
> The recipe for Sweet Japanese Pickles makes a total of 14 ounces (400 g) of assorted vegetables, making more pickles than you will need for a single batch of Colorful Sweet Pickle Sushi. This recipe saves you from working with impossibly small quantities of each ingredient, but it also means that you will have some pickles left over. Not to worry—these sweet pickles will keep for several days in your refrigerator, and they make a colorful side dish even as part of a non sushi meal. And by the way, feel free to substitute your own favorite homemade pickles for the ones listed here.

AVOCADO SESAME ROLLS

These dainty delights combine the creamy richness of pureed avocado with the smoky crunchiness of sesame seeds and the chewy tanginess of sushi rice—an amazing variety of sensations for a single bite.

Time 20 minutes plus 1 hour for rice preparation
Makes 8 pieces

½ **standard quantity Basic Sushi Rice (page 23)**
3 **tablespoons black sesame seeds**
1 **avocado**
½ **teaspoon lemon juice**
Dash of soy sauce
Chervil or parsley for garnish

❶ Prepare the Basic Sushi Rice.

❷ Cover a bamboo mat with plastic wrap. Shape the Basic Sushi Rice into an 8-inch (20-cm)-long bar in the center of the mat. Roll the mat up and tighten it to make the bar's thickness even.

❸ Sprinkle the sesame seeds on a plate, and roll the bar of rice back and forth over the seeds until it is well coated. Cut into 8 pieces.

❹ Separate the avocado from its pit and skin. Process the flesh of the fruit in a food processor until smooth. Add the lemon juice and soy sauce.

❺ Top each piece of the sesame-coated rice with a dollop of the avocado paste. Decorate with the chervil or parsley.

SPICY TUNA SESAME ROLLS

Although little known in Japan, spicy tuna is a sushi flavor that has caught on like wildfire worldwide. Combining the smooth caress of fresh tuna on your tongue with the sharp bite of chili pepper on your taste buds, this is a taste combination that deserves more attention. Fittingly, then, this recipe puts spicy tuna on a pedestal—a pedestal made of rice and sesame seeds, that is.

Time 20 minutes plus 1 hour for rice preparation
Makes 8 pieces

½ **standard quantity Basic Sushi Rice (page 23)**
3 **tablespoons white sesame seeds, roasted**
3½ **oz (85 g) fresh tuna, chopped**
1 **teaspoon chili paste**
Dash of soy sauce, or to taste
Chervil or parsley for garnish

❶ Prepare the Basic Sushi Rice.

❷ Cover a bamboo mat with plastic wrap. Shape the Basic Sushi Rice into an 8-inch (20-cm)-long bar in the center of the mat. Roll the mat up and tighten it to make the bar's thickness even.

❸ Sprinkle the sesame seeds on a plate, and roll the bar of rice back and forth over the seeds until it is well coated. Cut the bar into 8 pieces and lay them on their sides on a serving plate.

❹ Put the tuna, chili paste and soy sauce in a food processor and process until smooth.

❺ Top each sesame-coated portion of rice with a dollop of the spicy tuna paste. Garnish with chervil or parsley.

LAYERED VEGETABLE SUSHI

Oshi sushi, or pressed sushi, is the oldest style of sushi still widely eaten in Japan. Many varieties of oshi sushi exist, including this layered dish that resembles an elegant vegetable terrine. Pressed sushi is traditionally prepared in a boxlike wooden mold, but any container will do. In this case, a pound cake pan is just the thing.

Time 50 minutes plus 1 hour for rice preparation
Makes 1 loaf or 8 pieces

1 standard quantity Basic Sushi Rice (page 23)
1 small carrot
1 cup (250 ml) dashi broth
1 tablespoon sugar
½ teaspoon salt
3½ oz (85 g) snow peas

MINCED SHIITAKE
6 dried shiitake mushrooms, soaked in 2 cups (500 ml) water for several hours
1 cup (250 ml) water reserved from soaking mushrooms
1 tablespoon mirin
1 tablespoon sugar
1½ tablespoons soy sauce

SHREDDED EGGS
2 eggs
2 teaspoons mirin
2 teaspoons sugar
Pinch of salt
Vegetable oil

❶ Prepare the Basic Sushi Rice.

❷ Prepare the Minced Shiitake by soaking the shiitake mushrooms in 2 cups (500 ml) of water for at least 1 hour, but preferably overnight, until they are tender. Remove and discard the knobby root ends of the mushrooms' stems and mince the mushrooms very finely. In a pan, combine the shiitake, 1 cup of the water in which they have been soaking in, mirin, sugar and soy sauce. Bring the mixture to a boil, then lower the heat to its lowest setting and cook until the liquid is nearly all absorbed.

❸ Peel the carrot and cut into tiny pieces. Combine the carrot, dashi, sugar and salt in a pan and bring to a boil. Reduce the heat to its lowest setting and cook for a few minutes until the carrot is tender. Drain it when done.

❹ Finely chop the snow peas and boil them for 1 minute in salted water until tender. Drain them when done.

❺ Prepare the Shredded Eggs by mixing together the eggs, mirin, sugar and salt. Heat a egg pan or skillet and oil it lightly. Pour in just enough of the egg mixture to cover the bottom of the pan. When the egg starts to dry, turn it out onto a plate. Oil the pan again and repeat the same process until all of the egg mixture is used up. Shred the sheets of cooked egg into very fine pieces.

❻ Line a 3½ x 7 inch (9 x 18 cm) mini pound cake pan, about 2½ inches (6 cm) deep, with plastic wrap. Divide the Basic Sushi Rice into four portions and layer the first ¼ of it evenly over the bottom of the pan. Tamp it down with a flat tool such as the bottom of glass. (Moisten the tool to prevent rice from sticking.)

❼ Sprinkle the cooked carrot over the rice, forming a layer that touches the sides of the pan so that the color will show when turned out.

❽ Spread another ¼ of the rice over the carrots, and tamp down again. Sprinkle the snow peas in to create the next layer.

❾ Spread another ¼ of the rice over the snow peas, and tamp down again. Sprinkle the Minced Shiitake in to create the next layer.

❿ Spread the final ¼ of the rice over the mushrooms, and tamp down again, pressing rather firmly this time. Turn the molded sushi onto a serving plate. Top it with the finely shredded egg sheets. Cut into slices to serve.

RATATOUILLE SUSHI

Savory French ratatouille plus Japanese sushi rice add up to a tempting vegetarian treat. Note that while conventional ratatouille may be quite chunky, this recipe calls for the vegetables to be minced well so you can enjoy a little of everything in each bite.

½ standard quantity Basic Sushi Rice (page 23)
1 tablespoon olive oil
1 clove garlic, finely minced
½ onion, chopped
2 ripe tomatoes, seeded and chopped
1 Japanese eggplant, stem removed, minced
½ yellow bell pepper, stem and seeds removed, minced
½ teaspoon ground cumin
Salt and pepper to taste
8 to 12 broccoli or other sprouts for garnish

❶ Prepare the Basic Sushi Rice.

❷ To make the ratatouille, combine the oil and garlic in a pan. Cook the garlic until it begins to give off a good aroma. Add the onion and cook for 1 minute. Then add rest of the vegetables, cover and cook over low heat for about 10 minutes.

❸ Add the cumin and season with the salt and pepper.

❹ Moisten a mold of any shape that appeals to you and press ½ of the Basic Sushi Rice into it. Turn the rice out onto a serving plate, and repeat with the remaining rice on a second plate.

❺ Arrange the ratatouille over the molded rice portions. Sprinkle with the sprouts and serve.

Time 30 minutes plus 1 hour for rice preparation   **Makes** 2 servings

SUKIYAKI SUSHI

Japanese crooner Kyu Sakamoto's song "Sukiyaki," a worldwide hit in the 1960s, had nothing to do with the dish that shares its name. The original Japanese title, "Ue o Muite Aruko" (which means "walking along looking up at the sky"), was deemed too difficult for Westerners to pronounce, so "Sukiyaki" was chosen as a simpler international alternative. Even so, it is a dish worth singing about. The beef, onion and noodles are hearty fare, the dark sauce is both sweet and savory, and the fat content gives it a luscious mouthfeel.

½ standard quantity Basic Sushi
  Rice (page 23)
4 oz (100 g) fresh shirataki noodles
  or boiled harusame (cellophane
  noodles)
Salt for noodle preparation (optional)
1 tablespoon vegetable oil or
  beef fat
1 Japanese leek (naganegi), cut into
  2-in (5-cm) lengths
7 oz (200 g) beef loin, very thinly
  sliced
1½ tablespoons sugar
2 tablespoons sake
2 tablespoons water
3 tablespoons mirin
3 tablespoons soy sauce
Dash of ichimi togarashi (red
  pepper powder) or ground red
  pepper (cayenne) (optional)

❶ Prepare the Basic Sushi Rice.

❷ Prepare the shirataki noodles by removing them from their package and draining and rinsing them. To reduce any odor, massage the noodles with salt, and rinse again.

❸ Divide the Basic Sushi Rice into 6 portions. Place each portion into a moistened mold in your choice of shape and turn out onto a plate.

❹ In a pan, heat the oil or melt the beef fat. Cook the leek over high heat until slightly softened. Then add the beef slices. When the beef is barely cooked, add the shirataki noodles, the sugar and all of the liquid ingredients. Reduce the heat and cook until the liquid is mostly absorbed.

❺ Using chopsticks or your fingers, place the cooked ingredients on top of the molded rice. Top with a light dash of ichimi togarashi or ground red pepper, if desired.

Time 40 minutes plus 1 hour for rice preparation   **Makes** 6 pieces

CHAPTER FIVE

GLOBAL SUSHI

The appeal of sushi—delicious, healthy and attractively presented—may be obvious to you, but if you live outside of Japan you probably know at least a few people for whom sushi is still a foreign concept. If you'd like to try to win them over, the recipes in this chapter are one good place to start. Incorporating elements of great cuisines from around the world, these recipes feature fare that may be more familiar to them, such as British roast beef, German Wiener schnitzel or Korean kimchi.

This chapter includes more than a dozen recipes that I have created in the course of exploring and experimenting with dishes from around the globe. In some cases I have married sushi rice with international dishes that traditionally use rice of another kind, such as the pilaf I fondly remember from my childhood years spent in India, or the Hainanese chicken rice I have enjoyed so much on my visits to Singapore.

Spanish paella was a third international rice dish to inspire me, especially since it incorporates such an enticing variety of seafood, just as traditional sushi does. Spicy shrimp from Thailand is another world seafood treat that can be given the sushi treatment.

Of course, it should be clear by now that sushi does not absolutely have to include seafood, which is why this chapter also features my recipes for Peking Duck Sushi, the sauce for which may be prepared with either a Chinese or Japanese taste, and a Sausage and Cabbage Roll that is touched by the warmth of French mustard rather than by the fire of Japanese wasabi. Further flights of fancy include sushi riffs on such world favorites as French baguettes, Vietnamese spring rolls, Mexican tacos and even Italian pizza.

Of course, one can't get too carried away. Not just anything thrown together with some rice equals sushi. Good sushi rice is the heart and soul of real sushi, and even with these very innovative recipes you should make sure that your rice is properly prepared.

But with that in mind, sushi and the world's cuisines can unite to make a global culinary harmony. And the results may just help you turn that sushi skeptic among your family or friends into a sushi lover.

VIETNAMESE RICE PAPER SUSHI ROLLS

Spring rolls, usually deep-fried, are found in many Asian countries. But non-fried Thai and Vietnamese spring rolls—often referred to as "summer rolls"—made with soft, fresh, rice paper wrappers are just as tasty and even healthier to eat. The wrappers can be purchased ready-made at an Asian grocery or gourmet shop. This recipe makes two kinds of summer rolls—tuna and shrimp—that also have sushi rice inside to soak up the pungent fish sauce that is served in place of soy sauce for dipping.

Time 30 minutes plus 1 hour for rice preparation
Makes 12 pieces

1 standard quantity Basic Sushi Rice (page 23)
3 spring onions or thin green onions (scallions), finely chopped
4 tablespoons finely diced almonds
12 fresh rice paper spring roll wrappers
24 fresh coriander (cilantro) leaves
3 oz (90 g) fresh tuna, cut into 6 strips
1 tablespoon wasabi
1 avocado, thinly sliced
3 medium shrimp
About 1 tablespoon sake
Fish sauce, preferably Vietnamese (nuac mam), for dipping

❶ Prepare the Basic Sushi Rice. Mix the chopped spring onions and almonds into the rice. Divide the rice into 12 small portions.

❷ Lightly rinse a rice paper spring roll wrapper and pat it dry with a paper towel. Lay the wrapper on a wooden board. To make a tuna summer roll, place two coriander leaves horizontally in the center of the wrapper. Lay a slice of tuna, a little bit of wasabi and a slice of avocado on top of the leaves. Top these with a portion of the sushi rice, shaping it to fit the size of the tuna.

❸ Wrap the ingredients tightly to form a summer roll. To do this, fold the near side of the wrapper over the ingredients. Then, fold the left and right sides of the wrapper inward. Finally, roll the sushi away from you over the remaining loose part of the wrapper. Repeat the process to make a total of 6 tuna summer rolls.

❹ Shell and rinse the shrimp and cook them sakamushi style—that is, steamed in sake. Pour just enough sake to cover the bottom of a pan— about a tablespoon—plus a little water and a pinch of salt. Add the shrimp and bring the pot to a boil. Reduce the heat to medium and cook, covered, for a few minutes until the shrimp have a nice pink color. Be careful not to scorch or overcook them. You may also microwave the shrimp for 2 minutes with one tablespoon of sake in a dish covered with plastic wrap.

❺ To make the shrimp summer rolls, cut each shrimp in half lengthwise. Arrange the coriander leaves, a piece of shrimp, avocado, and sushi rice on a rice paper wrapper and roll them up just as described for the tuna summer rolls in steps 2 and 3. Repeat to make a total of 6 shrimp summer rolls.

❻ Serve the rolls whole or cut in two, with fish sauce on the side.

CABBAGE AND SAUSAGE SUSHI ROLLS

A mix of European flavors are imported into the sushi world in this dish, which combines German sausages with French mustard. In this recipe, Simple White Rice gets its sushi tang from the vinegary pickling brine of the gherkins that are served as an accompaniment.

Time 20 minutes plus 45 minutes for rice preparation
Makes 8 rolls

1 standard quantity Simple White Rice (page 25)
2 tablespoons pickling brine from a jar of gherkins
4 or 5 sprigs fresh dill, finely chopped
8 cabbage leaves
3 tablespoons Dijon or other mustard, preferably with seeds
8 German or other sausages, 1-in (2.5-cm) thick and 4 to 5 inches (10 to 12 cm) long
8 gherkin pickles

❶ Prepare the Simple White Rice.

❷ Mix the pickling brine with the rice. The flavor of the brine varies from brand to brand, so adjust the amount to suit your taste. Mix the dill into the rice, and divide the rice into 8 portions.

❸ Boil the cabbage leaves for a few minutes, until tender. Drain them and cut away the hard part of each leaf's rib, near the stem.

❹ Place a bamboo mat on a cutting board. Place one cabbage leaf on the mat, with the leaf's stem end toward you. In the center, spread one portion of the rice to cover an area measuring about the length of a sausage horizontally and 3 inches (8 cm) vertically.

❺ Spread some mustard across the center of the rice. Place a sausage on top. Fold the loose sides of the leaf inward and roll it up tightly with the mat.

❻ Remove the cabbage roll from the mat and cut in half to serve. Repeat with the remaining ingredients to make 8 rolls. Serve them with the gherkins on the side.

PEKING DUCK SUSHI

One of China's most famous dishes gets the sushi treatment in this recipe, which your guests can assemble at the table by rolling up duck meat and sushi rice in a Chinese pancake. You may opt to give it a slightly more Chinese or slightly more Japanese flavor by choosing between miso paste and hoisin sauce in the Sweet Peking Miso Sauce.

Time 30 minutes plus 1 hour for rice preparation
Makes 10 rolls

1 standard quantity Basic Sushi Rice (page 23)
1 Japanese cucumber
1½ teaspoons vegetable oil
1 duck breast or thigh, about 10 oz (300 g)
1 tablespoon sake
1 tablespoon soy sauce
½ tablespoon sugar
1 tablespoon plus 1 teaspoon mirin
1 Japanese leek (naganegi), about 9-in (23-cm) long
10 Chinese pancakes or fresh rice paper spring roll wrappers

SWEET PEKING MISO SAUCE

2 tablespoons miso paste or hoisin sauce
2 tablespoons water
½ tablespoon sugar
1 teaspoon soy sauce

① Prepare the Basic Sushi Rice.

② Using a vegetable peeler, slice several long, flat ribbons from the cucumber. Continue to slice away ribbons until ⅔ of the cucumber is used up. Soak the ribbons in ice water until crisp. Finely dice the remaining cucumber, and mix the diced portion into the Basic Sushi Rice.

③ Heat the oil in a skillet, and brown the skin side of the duck over medium-high heat. When nicely browned, turn the meat over and lower the heat. Cover and cook until done, for about 5 minutes.

④ Add the sake, soy sauce, sugar and 1 tablespoon of the mirin to the skillet. Cook the duck over medium-high heat until all the liquid is absorbed, turning the meat several times while cooking. Add the remaining teaspoon of mirin and cook briskly until the duck takes on a nice glossy look. Remove the duck from the heat and allow it to cool.

⑤ Prepare thin, crisp onion strips (called shiraganegi, meaning "white hair onion," in Japanese) by cutting the Japanese leek into 3-inch (7-cm) lengths. Make a deep vertical cut in each piece and remove the core in the center. Open the leek and flatten it out on a cutting board. Piling a few leek sheets on top of each other, slice them very finely, following the grain. Soak the resulting strips in ice water for a few minutes, until crisp. (*Note*: If you can't find Japanese leek, one bunch of spring onions or green onions can be substituted here, although cutting them up is more labor-intensive.)

⑥ Slice the duck and arrange it on a serving plate with the leek. Arrange the rice on another plate, garnishing it with the cucumber strips.

⑦ Prepare the Sweet Peking Miso Sauce by mixing all of the ingredients in a bowl and microwaving them for 1 minute.

⑧ Prepare the Chinese pancakes or fresh rice paper spring roll wrappers as directed on their package. Serve the rice, duck and pancakes with Sweet Peking Miso Sauce on the side. Allow your guest to roll up the various ingredients in the pancakes or wrappers as they like.

THAI SHRIMP SUSHI PARCELS

The sweet, hot and savory flavors of Thailand are echoed in this dish, which combines pineapples, chili and the nation's famous nam pla fish sauce with shrimp. As a final touch, chopped cashew nuts add some crunchy texture.

Time 20 minutes, plus 1 hour for rice preparation
Serves 2 to 3 people

1 standard quantity Basic Sushi Rice (page 23)
4 to 5 oz (about 125 g) fresh small shrimp, shelled and deveined
Dash of salt
1 tablespoon sake
½ teaspoon chili sauce
1 teaspoon fish sauce, preferably Thai (nam pla)
⅔ cup (60 g) finely diced pineapple (either fresh or canned)
2 tablespoons roasted and finely chopped cashew nuts
4 or 5 fresh lettuce leaves
1 fresh chili pepper, thinly sliced
4 or 5 sprigs fresh coriander (cilantro)

❶ Prepare the Basic Sushi Rice.

❷ In a microwave-safe dish, combine the shrimp, salt and sake. Cover the dish with plastic wrap and microwave it for few minutes until the shrimp are just done. Drain the shrimp, but reserve 1 tablespoon of the liquid.

❸ Add the chili sauce and fish sauce to the liquid from the shrimp. Mix it into the Basic Sushi Rice.

❹ Add the pineapples and cashew nuts to the rice and mix gently but thoroughly.

❺ Line several small serving bowls or other small containers with the lettuce leaves and turn the rice out into them. Top each of the rice "parcels" with the cooked shrimp and garnish with the sliced chili pepper and fresh coriander.

SINGAPORE CHICKEN RICE SUSHI

Inspired by Singapore's beloved Hainanese chicken rice, this recipe gets its sunny flavor from ginger, and its zesty energy from a homemade Chili Sauce. This is a good dish for sushi beginners, as it has the least acidic rice. Those who want a little more can supply their own with the accompanying lemon wedges.

Time 40 minutes plus 30 minutes
to soak rice
Serves 4 to 5 people

2 cups (400 g) uncooked rice
2 boneless chicken thighs, about
    1 to 1½ lbs (450 to 700 grams)
Salt
One 4-in (10-cm)-long piece
    Japanese leek (naganegi) or
    green onion (scallion), chopped
3 thin slices fresh ginger
2½ cups (625 ml) water
2 tablespoons lemon juice
½ cucumber, finely diced
4 sprigs fresh coriander (cilantro)
4 lemon wedges

CHILI SAUCE
7 oz (200 g) stewed tomatoes
4 tablespoons vinegar
3 tablespoons sugar
½ to 1 teaspoon dried red pepper
    flakes
1 teaspoon soy sauce

❶ Thoroughly wash the rice, rinsing it until the water runs clear, and then soak it in water for at least 30 minutes. Drain.

❷ Trim excess fat from the chicken. Cut the meat to a uniform thickness for even cooking. Sprinkle the chicken with salt. Place the chicken, chopped leek, ginger and water in a pot and bring to a boil. Cover the pot, lower the heat and let it simmer for 15 minutes until done. Set the chicken aside to cool and strain the broth.

❸ In a pan, bring 2 cups (500 ml) of the broth and ½ teaspoon of salt to a boil. Add the drained rice. Stir, cover and bring to a boil once again. Lower the heat and cook for 10 more minutes. Remove from the heat, mix in the lemon juice and the cucumber, and let it stand for 5 minutes.

❹ To prepare the Chili Sauce, combine the tomatoes, vinegar, sugar, dried red pepper flakes and soy sauce in a blender or food processor. Puree until smooth, and then pour the mixture into a pan and cook until it is slightly thickened.

❺ Serve the rice with the chicken pieces on top and Chili Sauce on the side. Garnish with the coriander and lemon wedges.

PAELLA SUSHI

At opposite ends of Eurasia, two different peoples—the Japanese and the Spanish—came up with different versions of the same great idea. The Japanese combined rice and seafood to make sushi, while the Spanish combined rice and seafood to make paella. The star ingredients of paella—squid and shrimp—are popular in both countries. The logical next step is to combine it all, and make Paella Sushi. For a dramatic presentation, you may choose to leave the heads on the shrimp.

Time 30 minutes plus 30 minutes to
   soak rice and mussels
Serves 4 to 6 people

2 cups (400 g) uncooked rice
8 live mussels
5 medium shrimp
1 medium squid, body about
   8-in (20-cm) long, head and legs
   removed
2 cups (500 ml) chicken stock
1 teaspoon saffron
Heaping ½ teaspoon salt
½ red bell pepper
½ green bell pepper
1 medium onion, diced
1 lemon, cut into wedges
2 tablespoons fresh chopped
   parsley

TOMATO DRESSING
2 tablespoon white wine vinegar
1 tablespoon lemon juice
1½ teaspoons sugar
½ teaspoon salt
2 tablespoons water
1 tablespoon olive oil
2 tablespoons finely minced onion
3 oz (80 g) coarsely chopped
   tomatoes

❶ Rinse the rice until the water runs clear, and then soak it for at least 30 minutes.

❷ Place the live mussels in a pot or bowl of fresh water for at least 20 minutes. During this time, they should naturally expel any sand or dirt inside. After removing them from the water, cut or pull off their stringy beards, and scrub away any other external dirt.

❸ Devein the shrimp.

❹ Clean the squid, pulling out the stiff, translucent cuttlebone, and thoroughly rinsing the interior. Then peel off the membranous skin. (Start by making a knife incision where the fins or "wings" meet the body.) Cut the squid's tubular body into rings about ¼-inch (6-mm) thick.

❺ Bring the stock to a boil in a paella pan or a skillet and add the saffron and salt. Add the drained rice, stir, and arrange the mussels, shrimp, squid rings and vegetables on the surface of the rice.

❻ Cover the pot and cook for 10 minutes over low heat. Remove the pot from the heat and let it stand, covered for 5 minutes. Sprinkle with the chopped parsley.

❼ Mix all the ingredients for the Tomato Dressing, being sure to add them in exactly the order they are listed.

❽ Serve the paella with the sauce on the side.

TACO SUSHI

The Japanese word for taco is pronounced "tacos." This helps avoid confusion with "tako," the Japanese word for octopus. But there is no octopus in this whimsical variation of the popular Mexican dish—just lime-flavored sushi rice, spicy ground beef, and fresh lettuce, tomatoes and cheese. If you like to wash down your tacos with beer, then Japanese Sapporo or Mexican Corona will do equally well.

Time 30 minutes plus 45 minutes for rice preparation
Makes 6 to 8 tacos

1 standard quantity Simple White Rice (page 25)
2 tablespoons lime juice
2 oz (50 g) cheese, cut into ¼-in (6-mm) dice
1½ teaspoons olive oil
1 clove garlic, minced
½ lb (250 g) ground beef
4 tablespoons tomato ketchup
A few drops Tabasco or other hot sauce to taste
Salt and pepper to taste
3 leaves crisp iceberg lettuce, finely shredded
6 to 10 cherry tomatoes, chopped
6 to 8 taco shells

❶ Prepare the Simple White Rice.

❷ Add the lime juice to the rice and mix well. Add the cheese and mix well. Divide the rice into 6 to 8 roughly equal portions, depending on the number of tacos you wish to make.

❸ Combine the oil and garlic in a pan, and cook over medium heat until the garlic is lightly browned. Add the ground beef and stir until the meat is cooked.

❹ Add the ketchup and Tabasco sauce and season with the salt and pepper.

❺ Spoon one portion of the rice into each taco shell along with some shredded lettuce and cooked beef. Sprinkle the chopped tomatoes on top and serve immediately. Alternatively, arrange the rice, vegetables and meat on a platter and allow your guests to build their own tacos at the table. This will help keep the taco shells crisp until they are ready to be eaten.

KOREAN KIMCHI & PORK SUSHI ROLLS

Japanese sushi rolls have Korean cousins known as "kimpa." The essence of this dish is rice rolled in a sheet of nori seaweed, but while sushi rice is prepared with vinegar, kimpa rice is mixed with sesame oil. This recipe puts Basic Sushi Rice and sesame oil together, and then adds another Korean treat—kimchi, the spicy pickled vegetables (usually Chinese cabbage) that are becoming more popular around the world.

Time 30 minutes plus 1 hour for rice preparation
Makes 2 rolls

1 standard quantity Basic Sushi Rice (page 23)
1½ tablespoons dark sesame oil
2 oz (50 g) pork loin, thinly sliced
2 eggs
½ cucumber, thinly sliced
Salt and pepper
2 sheets nori seaweed, about 7 x 8 in (18 x 20 cm)
3 oz (80 g) kimchi, cut into 1-in (2.5-cm) pieces

❶ Prepare the Basic Sushi Rice.

❷ Add 1 tablespoon of the sesame oil to the Basic Sushi Rice. Mix gently but thoroughly.

❸ Heat the remaining ½ tablespoon of sesame oil in a skillet. Sprinkle salt and pepper on the pork slices, and stir-fry them until the pork turns white. Slightly beat the eggs and add them to the skillet, along with the cucumber. Season the mixture to taste with a little salt and pepper. When the egg is nearly done, remove the pan from the heat.

❹ Place a sheet of nori on a bamboo mat on a board. Spread ½ of the rice evenly on the nori, leaving a 1-inch (2.5-cm) strip of uncovered nori on the side farthest from you.

❺ Lightly squeeze or press the kimchi to remove excess water. Arrange ½ of the kimchi across the center of the rice. Arrange ½ of the pork and egg mixture on the kimchi. Roll it up tightly in the mat. Remove the roll from the mat and cut it into slices. Repeat with the remaining ingredients to make another roll.

SHRIMP RICE PILAF SUSHI

This Indian-influenced chirashi sushi mixed sushi dish is topped with curry-marinated shrimp, and accompanied by a mildly spicy yogurt sauce.

Time 30 minutes plus 30 minutes to soak rice
Serves 4 to 5 people

2 cups (400 g) uncooked rice
12 medium shrimp
2 cups (500 ml) water
1 tablespoon curry powder
½ teaspoon salt
½ cup (75 g) green peas
1 tablespoon lemon juice
4 sprigs fresh coriander (cilantro)

SHRIMP MARINADE

3 tablespoons plain yogurt
1 teaspoon curry powder
½ teaspoon garam masala
1 teaspoon salt

YOGURT SAUCE

½ cup (125 g) plain yogurt
1 tablespoon sugar
½ tablespoon ketchup
½ teaspoon cumin
½ teaspoon curry powder
½ teaspoon salt
1 teaspoon sugar (optional, according to sourness of the yogurt)

❶ Wash the rice, and soak it for at least 30 minutes. Drain.

❷ Wash, shell and devein the shrimp.

❸ Prepare the Shrimp Marinade by mixing the yogurt, curry powder, garam masala and salt. Marinate the shrimp in this mixture for about 10 minutes.

❹ In a pan, combine the water with the curry powder and salt. When it comes to a boil, add the rice and peas. Stir, cover the pot, and bring it to a boil again. Remove the shrimp from the marinade and add them to the rice pot. (Do not stir them in—just let them cook on the surface of the rice.) Cover, reduce the heat to its lowest setting, and cook for 10 minutes.

❺ Prepare the Yogurt Sauce by mixing all of the ingredients in a bowl. Depending on the sourness of the yogurt you are using, you may want to add a little less or a little more sugar.

❻ When the rice is done, take out the shrimp and set them aside. Gently mix the lemon juice into the rice. Serve the rice on a plate, with the shrimp arranged on top. Garnish it with the coriander and serve the Yogurt Sauce on the side.

TONKATSU PORK CUTLET SUSHI

There are restaurants in every corner of Japan that specialize exclusively in tonkatsu, or breaded pork cutlets. This ubiquitous Japanese meal actually has Germanic roots, as a pork variation of Wiener schnitzel, a breaded veal dish. Tonkatsu is typically enjoyed with a dark, thick, tangy sauce, with numerous types commercially available. This recipe also includes a tip on whipping up your own Tonkatsu Sauce by combining tomato ketchup and balsamic vinegar.

Time 40 minutes plus 1 hour for rice preparation
Makes 10 pieces

1 standard quantity Basic Sushi Rice (page 23)
1 tablespoon Dijon mustard with seeds
1 teaspoon salt
½ teaspoon vegetable oil
8 to 10 fresh lettuce leaves
2 cups (500 ml) vegetable oil for deep-frying
7 oz (200 g) pork fillets, cut into 10 small pieces
Dash of salt and pepper to season the pork fillets
½ cup (65 g) all-purpose flour
1 egg, lightly beaten
1 cup (125 g) breadcrumbs

TONKATSU SAUCE

2 tablespoons balsamic vinegar
2 tablespoons tomato ketchup

❶ Prepare the Basic Sushi Rice. Add the mustard to the rice and mix well.

❷ Boil some water in a pan. Add 1 teaspoon of salt and ½ teaspoon of vegetable oil. Blanch the lettuce leaves and then immediately soak them in iced water. Drain the leaves and blot excess water from them with paper towel or tea towel. This process should result in lettuce leaves that are pliable and shiny.

❸ Cover a bamboo mat with a sheet of plastic wrap. Arrange ½ of the lettuce leaves on the mat overlapping each other to cover an area about 6 inches (15 cm) square, a little smaller than a standard sheet of nori. (To avoid soggy results, be sure there is no excess water on the lettuce.)

❹ Arrange ½ of the rice like a log across the center of the lettuce. Use the mat to roll up the rice inside the lettuce, and tighten it to form a firm roll. (Optionally, you may flatten the sides of the rolled-up mat to give the sushi roll a square-shaped cross-section.) Unroll the mat and remove the plastic wrap. Then, drape the roll with plastic wrap and cut it into 5 slices. Repeat with the remaining rice and lettuce to make a second roll.

❺ Arrange the sliced sushi on a platter, with a cut side up. Cover it with a thin, damp cloth to keep it from drying out.

❻ Start to warm the 2 cups (500 ml) of oil in a deep pan for deep-frying. Cut the pork fillets into 10 small pieces. Sprinkle them with salt and pepper. Dredge them in the flour, then the beaten egg and then the breadcrumbs. Deep-fry the small cutlets in 350°F (175°C) oil for few minutes until done. Set the meat on a rack or paper towel to allow excess oil to drain.

❼ Prepare the Tonkatsu Sauce by mixing together the balsamic vinegar and tomato ketchup in a small bowl. Top each piece of sliced sushi with a petite pork cutlet. Serve with the Tonkatsu Sauce on the side.

SUSHI PIZZAS

At first glance, Italian pizza and Japanese sushi may not seem to have much in common, but one characteristic they share is a remarkable versatility. This recipe, a sushi tribute to pizza, results in two lovely little "pies." One of them follows the classic Margherita theme of cheese, tomatoes and basil, while the other goes for a more modern sensibility with an abundance of leafy green salad.

Time 30 minutes (for each kind of pizza) plus 45 minutes for rice preparation
Makes 2 pies

1 standard quantity Simple White Rice (page 25)
1 tablespoon lemon juice

MARGHERITA PIZZA SUSHI

½ tablespoon olive oil
Dash of Italian herb mix (oregano, thyme and basil, etc.)
½ cup (100 g) strained pureed tomatoes
Dash of salt and pepper
1½ oz (40 g) shredded mozzarella cheese
1 fresh medium tomato, sliced
6 or 7 fresh basil leaves

SALAD-STYLE PIZZA SUSHI

½ tablespoon olive oil
1½ oz (40 g) shredded mozzarella cheese
1 oz (30 g) rocket leaves
1 oz (30 g) baby red cabbage leaves
3 slices prosciutto ham

PIZZA SALAD DRESSING

2 tablespoons rice vinegar
2 tablespoons pale sesame oil
½ tablespoon white sesame seeds, roasted
2 teaspoons sugar
2 teaspoons soy sauce

❶ Prepare the Simple White Rice.

❷ Gently mix the lemon juice into the rice.

❸ Preheat the oven to 400°F (200°C).

❹ Divide the rice into 2 portions. Shape each portion into a ball and then roll it flat with a rolling pin to form an 8-inch (18-cm) circle. To keep the rolling pin from sticking, drape the rice with plastic wrap. Place each circle of rice on an ovenproof dish. With your fingers, pinch the edges of each circle to create a raised border barely ½ inch (1.25 cm) higher than the center.

❺ For the Margherita Pizza Sushi, sprinkle one circle with the olive oil. Combine the Italian herbs with the pureed tomatoes and spread them on top of the olive oil. Sprinkle the circle with the salt, pepper and mozzarella cheese. Arrange the tomato slices on top. Bake the pizza sushi in the preheated oven for 15 minutes, until crispy. Remove from the oven and garnish with the basil leaves.

❻ For the Salad-style Pizza Sushi, sprinkle the second rice circle with its portion of the olive oil, and then the cheese. Bake for 15 minutes until crispy. Top with the rocket leaves, baby red cabbage and prosciutto.

❼ Mix together the ingredients for the Pizza Salad Dressing and serve the dressing alongside.

BAGUETTE SUSHI

Fresh tomatoes and ripe Camembert cheese team up as an ideal filling for a French baguette sandwich. In this homage to Parisian bistro cuisine, tomatoes and cheese prove that they go well together on sushi, too. Bon appetit!

Time 20 minutes plus 1 hour for rice preparation
Makes 8 baguettes

1 standard quantity Brown Sushi Rice (page 25)
4 pieces fried tofu (abura-age)
4½ oz (125 g) Camembert cheese, cut into ½-in (1.25-cm) pieces
4 cherry tomatoes, cut into wedges
4 to 8 sprigs fresh Italian parsley for garnish
Mixed green salad as a side dish

HONEY MUSTARD DRESSING

3 tablespoons olive oil
1 tablespoon white wine vinegar
1 teaspoon Dijon mustard with seeds
½ teaspoon salt
½ teaspoon soy sauce

① Prepare the Brown Sushi Rice.

② Cut each piece of abura-age in half vertically and open out each of the halves like a long, canoe-shaped purse. Fill each of them with ⅛ of the Brown Sushi Rice, gently molding them to achieve the look of a long baguette sandwich.

③ Decorate the top of the rice with the cheese.

④ Grill in a toaster oven until the fried tofu is brown and crisp. Garnish with the tomatoes and parsley.

⑤ Mix the ingredients for the Honey Mustard Dressing. Toss the mixed green salad with the dressing and serve on the side with the finished baguettes.

ACKNOWLEDGMENTS

Many people and organizations helped make this book a reality. I especially wish to thank:

Tom Baker, writer

Noboru Murata, photographer

Masami Kaneko, food stylist

Masayo Kanda, Ikuko Ito and Yumiko Nakano, cooking assistants

Shinsuke Suzuki, Kazuko Ikemoto and Taeko Kamei of Tuttle Publishing, Japan

Christina Oey, Eric Oey, Holly Jennings, Chan Sow Yun (designer) of Tuttle Publishing

Misawa Homes Co., Ltd , Time & Style Co. Ltd
Yoko Mizui

ABOUT THE WRITER

Tom Baker is a coauthor of the luxury travel guidebook *Tokyo Chic* and has also contributed to the *Time Out* guides to Tokyo. He has written about Japan for *Jaguar*, *Continental*, *Japan Close-up* and other magazines. He lives in Saitama Prefecture.

ABOUT THE STYLIST

Masami Kaneko is a versatile stylist whose work has been described as both lively and creative. The scope of her work ranges from advertising to editorial—including cookbooks, and interior design and food magazines—and includes consultation for wedding parties and restaurant table settings. She is based in Tokyo.

RESOURCE GUIDE

Japanese foods are becoming ever more widely available at supermarkets and specialty stores across the English-speaking world. And one of the most enjoyable ways to buy fish has always been to strike up a conversation with the person behind the seafood counter at your neighborhood grocery store or regional fish market to get informed recommendations about the catch of the day. But if you can't find what you need nearby, the Internet can be a great help, with a few mouse-clicks bringing the items you need straight to your door.

The following list is not meant as an endorsement of any particular business; it is provided merely as a reference to help you start looking:

United States
Amazon.com (has a lot of sushi-relevant items in its "Gourmet Food" section)
amazon.com

Asian Food Grocer (Japanese foods)
asianfoodgrocer.com

Catalina Offshore Products (seafood with an emphasis on sushi and sashimi)
catalinaop.com

eFoodDepot.com (online grocer with a Japan section)
facebook.com/efooddepotcom/

eKitron.com (Japanese cookware)
ekitron.com

House Foods America (tofu, noodles and spices)
house-foods.com

Melissa's (specialty produce dealer)
melissas.com

Mitsuwa Marketplace (Japanese foods)
mitsuwa.com

Specialty Produce (hard-to-find vegetables)
specialtyproduce.com

Sushi foods (sushi supplies)
sushifoods.com

Britain
Japan Centre (Japanese food and cookware)
japancentre.com

Japanese Kitchen (Japanese food and cookware)
japanesekitchen.co.uk

Mount Fuji (Japanese food and cookware)
mountfuji.co.uk

INDEX

"Books to Span the East and West"

Tuttle Publishing was founded in 1832 in the small New England town of Rutland, Vermont [USA]. Our core values remain as strong today as they were then—to publish best-in-class books which bring people together one page at a time. In 1948, we established a publishing office in Japan—and Tuttle is now a leader in publishing English-language books about the arts, languages and cultures of Asia. The world has become a much smaller place today and Asia's economic and cultural influence has grown. Yet the need for meaningful dialogue and information about this diverse region has never been greater. Over the past seven decades, Tuttle has published thousands of books on subjects ranging from martial arts and paper crafts to language learning and literature—and our talented authors, illustrators, designers and photographers have won many prestigious awards. We welcome you to explore the wealth of information available on Asia at **www.tuttlepublishing.com.**

Please note that the publisher and author(s) of this cookbook are NOT RESPONSIBLE in any manner whatsoever for any domestic accidents, fires, food poisoning or allergic reactions that could result from the preparation of the recipes given within, including from the eating of raw vegetables, eggs, meat and fish. The publisher and author(s) are not responsible for any kind of food borne disease or illness caused by undercooked food.

Published by Tuttle Publishing, an imprint of Periplus Editions (HK) Ltd.,

www.tuttlepublishing.com

Copyright © 2022 Periplus Editions (HK) Ltd

All rights reserved. No part of this publication may be reproduced or utilized in any form or by any means, electronic or mechanical, including photocopying, recording, or by any information storage and retrieval system, without prior written permission from the publisher.

ISBN 978-4-8053-1732-7
(Previously published under Isbn 978-4-8053-0915-5 [HC], LCCI No. 2008042077 & Isbn 978-4-8053-1299-5 [PB])

Distributed by
North America, Latin America & Europe
Tuttle Publishing
364 Innovation Drive
North Clarendon, VT 05759-9436 U.S.A.
Tel: 1 (802) 773-8930; Fax: 1 (802) 773-6993
info@tuttlepublishing.com
www.tuttlepublishing.com

Japan
Tuttle Publishing
Yaekari Building, 3rd Floor
5-4-12 Osaki, Shinagawa-ku
Tokyo 141 0032
Tel: (81) 3 5437-0171
Fax: (81) 3 5437-0755
sales@tuttle.co.jp
www.tuttle.co.jp

Asia Pacific
Berkeley Books Pte Ltd
3 Kallang Sector #04-01,
Singapore 349278.
Tel: (65) 6741-2178; Fax: (65) 6741-2179
inquiries@periplus.com.sg
www.tuttlepublishing.com

24 23 22   10 9 8 7 6 5 4 3 2 1

Printed in China   2207EP

TUTTLE PUBLISHING® is a registered trademark of Tuttle Publishing, a division of Periplus Editions (HK) Ltd.